Library of
Davidson College

Taxation — Dollars and Sense

THE M. L. SEIDMAN MEMORIAL
TOWN HALL LECTURE SERIES

MEMPHIS STATE UNIVERSITY

The M. L. Seidman Memorial Town Hall Lecture Series was established by P. K. Seidman in memory of his late brother, M. L. Seidman, founder of the firm Seidman and Seidman, Certified Public Accountants.

Publication of this fourth Series of Seidman Lectures was made possible by a gift from Mr. P. K. Seidman to the Memphis State University Press.

The M. L. Seidman Memorial Town Hall Lecture Series

1966-67	*Financial Policies in Transition,* edited by Dr. Thomas O. Depperschmidt.
1967-68	*The USSR in Today's World,* edited by Dr. Festus Justin Viser.
1968-69	*The News Media — A Service and a Force,* edited by Dr. Festus Justin Viser.

Taxation — Dollars and Sense

edited by Festus Justin Viser
Professor of Economics
Memphis State University

MEMPHIS STATE UNIVERSITY PRESS   1971

Copyright, 1971
By Memphis State University Press

All Rights Reserved

Library of Congress Catalog Card Number: 75-151266
ISBN 0-87870-007-2

Manufactured in the United States of America
by Paragon Press, Inc., Montgomery, Alabama

Contents

Preface vii

Lecture One 1
Taxation and Civilization in the Seventies
by Walter W. Heller

Lecture Two 27
The Role of Taxation in Meeting Social Problems
by Paul R. McDaniel

Lecture Three 73
How Can We Kick the Intaxication Habit
by J. S. Seidman

Coordinating Committee

FESTUS J. VISER, Director
    Professor of Economics
    Memphis State University

FRANK R. ALGREN
    Retired Editor
    Memphis Commercial Appeal

THE REVEREND ROBERT P. ATKINSON
    Rector
    Calvary Episcopal Church

RONALD E. CARRIER
    Vice President
    Memphis State University

S. L. KOPALD, JR.
    Executive Vice President
    Humko Products Division
    Kraftco Corporation

HERBERT J. MARKLE
    Dean
    School of Business Administration
    Memphis State University

MRS. ROLAND H. MYERS

D. A. NOEL
    General Manager
    WHBQ Radio-Television Station

P. K. SEIDMAN
    Partner
    Seidman and Seidman CPA

EARL H. TRIPLETT
    President
    Memphis Bank and Trust Company

Taxation — Dollars and Sense

Preface

A well-worn proverb instructs us that taxes are painful to pay and deadly to discuss. Deadly or not, the Seidman Coordinating Committee, after much deliberation, decided that taxation would be a lively subject in 1969 and into 1970.

In late 1968 and early 1969, the expression "a taxpayer's revolt" began to appear and to be discussed by some as a distinct possibility. I recall in late 1968, for example, being asked in a local television interview if I thought that a taxpayer's revolt was likely. I did not think so then; I do not now. I do think taxation is not so deadly a subject as we once thought.

One important reason for this is that over the last several decades taxation has become such a complicated subject. At one time, it was no more than a matter of paying the bills of government and distributing the resulting financial burden in some way that a democratic society would be willing to accept. But today taxes do things besides produce revenues. As a graduate student, I vividly recall hearing the distinguished George Stigler say that we have come to place so many burdens on the tax system that it is a wonder that it does not break down altogether.

For example, taxation plays a major role in stabilizing the economy. We have come to think of it as income redistributing, at least to the extent of having created our broad-based middle class in the United States. Lately we have been discussing it as a force, perhaps the "deus ex machina," for eliminating poverty. Thus would emerge the negative income tax. Some have decried our affluence as being characterized by an overabundance of private goods, existing side by side with a glaring, shame-faced poverty of social goods. Only properly ordered tax flows could be expected to cure this strange economic paradox.

In late April of 1969, President Nixon brought his tax reform proposal before the Congress. This was in conjunction with his request for the extension of the Johnson surtax — an anti-inflationary move that he badly needed. A tax reform bill was immediately introduced into the House, and the summer and fall struggle with this legislation is well-known history. The bill emerged from the Congressional Conference Committee on December 21 as the Tax Reform Bill of 1969. Although signed by the President on December 30, it was not the bill he had wanted, and almost certainly not the bill the general public wanted. It was enacted too rapidly. It was not sufficiently researched. It was not broadly and profoundly enough conceived. In fact, many of us hope that this Tax Reform Bill of 1969 will serve primarily as a launching pad for an era of tax study, and as the initial legislation in an era of tax reform.

The late Mr. M. L. Seidman, the man in whose memory our series has been established, was one of the nation's leading authorities on taxation. Throughout his life, Mr. Seidman maintained an active interest in this subject, and his expertise became widely recognized. Three New York State governors, Alfred Smith, Franklin D. Roosevelt, and Herbert Lehman, appointed him as their delegate to the National Taxation Association. Even so, the late Mr. Seidman felt that taxation was an issue for the general public, and in this connection, for many years wrote a taxation column that came to be syndicated in over one hundred newspapers.

One of his illustrious surviving brothers, Mr. J. S. Seidman, has diligently followed in his late brother's footsteps. He too has become an eminent authority on taxation. Some years ago he wrote and published a definitive volume, *Seidman's Legislative History on Federal Income and Excess Profits Tax Laws*. This work is in four volumes and runs to nearly 7,000 pages. Moreover, Mr. J. S. Seidman was a tax columnist for twenty-one years for the late *New York Herald Tribune*. Since its demise, his articles now appear in the *New York Times* and other national publications. Hardly a professional meeting of any scope on the issues of taxation is held that Mr. J. S. Seidman does not help plan, participate in as a speaker-lecturer, or more likely both.

It was generally agreed by the Coordinating Committee that the subject of the social uses of taxation would not be acceptable unless it included Walter W. Heller as one of its key participants — that economic advisor and personal confidant who so significantly and unprecedently influenced both President John F. Kennedy and President Lyndon B. Johnson to use taxation manipulation for the first time as a non-emergency fiscal tool. Dr. Heller had been an academic economist for many years at the University of Minnesota. He had written, mainly for his profession, but widely and challengingly. He came to President Kennedy as a novice public office holder with the complete respect and admiration of his fellow professional practitioners. History will recognize him as one of the founders of the so-called new economics: not so much a body of doctrine, but rather a format of policy that emphasizes growth targets for an economy and their achievement mainly through fiscal policy manipulations.

Dr. Heller chose to discuss: "Taxation and Civilization in the Seventies." This decade, beginning as it has with a surge of inflation, leads him to introduce several new dimensions to his new economics. Throughout his discussion, however, he remains the true economist — no political partisanship shows. His remarks are profound and thought-provoking. His essay is one that must be reread several times; for each reading seems to bring forth valuable new meaning and insight.

Another necessary participant was Paul R. McDaniel. After several years as Attorney Advisor in the Office of the Tax Legislative Council of the United States Treasury Department, he became a much discussed direct activist in the Tax Reform Bill of 1969 by shifting from that position in August of 1969, to Special Assistant on Tax Legislation to Senator Albert Gore. It will be recalled that Senator Gore fought diligently and doggedly for comprehensive tax reform when the bill finally reached the Senate. Mr. McDaniel represented a significant part of the facts, figures, and philosophy behind Senator Gore's dramatic effort in behalf of the bill.

Mr. McDaniel's paper is brilliant. He introduces a new concept, "the tax expenditure" as he terms it. With this ingenious conceptual device, we are led to view a tax deduction as the equivalent of a tax paid concurrent with a government outlay to the deduction taker. This establishes firm ground on which to view the rightness or wrongness of tax deduction.

It is in this context that Mr. McDaniel examines "The Role of Taxation in Meeting Social Problems." His essay is clear, lucid, and the new vantage points his innovative concept provide makes it an exciting piece of theoretical work. It is a real contribution to the volume.

Mr. Jacob S. Seidman was chosen to complete what the Committee hoped to be a roster blending authority

Seidman Lectures

with challenge. I have already told you of Mr. Seidman's background. His selected subject, "How to Kick the Intaxication Habit" intrigued everyone. But indeed, it proved to be substantially more than an amusing set of capricious, whimsical commentaries. Rather, it asks the key question so often avoided — how much government spending can a modern economy afford? Mr. Seidman's focus is on spending management and on achieving real and continuing tax economy through expert spending management.

These three documents make a substantial contribution to the literature on taxation. They are fresh and current — clearly focused on the problems of the years immediately before us.

There are so many people to whom I owe gratitude in helping me to bring this 1969-70 Series about. My Coordinating Committee gave me invaluable and much needed advice. It never ceased to be a source of encouragement. University staff people — the behind the scenes publicity people, conference services peoples, artists, printing shop personnel and the like — all deserve my praise and gratitude. Particular gratitude is extended to Mr. Robert T. Garnett, who assisted expertly with so many innumerable but vitally important details.

Mr. P. K. Seidman stood by me faithfully and loyally as he has done in the past. As I have said in previous editions, he truly memorializes his brother, because he gives his personal time, energy, and continuing interest, as well as his financial support. Memphis State University and the greater Memphis community reap a truly rich reward as the result of this concerned and dedicated gentleman.

Festus J. Viser
August, 1970

"Taxation and Civilization in the Nineteen Seventies"

Lecture One

by Walter W. Heller

Taxes are, as Justice Holmes reminded us, the price of civilization. And the price is going up. As civilization becomes more complex, more demanding, and more vulnerable, the demands on our tax system rise correspondingly. In part, the demand is for higher standards of economic performance, for a demonstration that — in spite of the lame and halting tax response to the inflation since 1966 — we have what it takes in political will and legislative ingenuity to train our tax guns as effectively on inflation in the Seventies as we did on slack and slow growth in the Sixties. In part, it is that taxes must do their part in meeting the categorical imperative of the Seventies, namely to re-channel America's affluence so as to redress the wrongs we have inflicted on man — on the poor, the ignorant, and the black — and on his environment — on our air, our water, and our land — an imperative that calls for greater tax effort, not less. In part, it is a call for higher standards of fairness and equity, both in the narrow sense of ending special tax shelters and privilege and in the broad sense of modifying the distribution of tax burdens, particularly with an eye to untaxing those below the poverty line. In part, it is the task of strengthening our federalism, of redressing its federal-state-local balance of revenues and power, of giving new and constructive substance to "states' rights," by forging new links in the intergovernmental tax chain through federal sharing and tax credits.

If I seem to be suggesting, among other things, that the tax cuts that helped the Sixties soar may have to be supplanted by tax increases to help make the Seventies heavenly, that is indeed so. But hear me out.

As we draw up our tax agenda for the Seventies, let's pause a moment to see where the Sixties have brought us. In 1970, once the 10% surtax has disappeared, we will be paying some $23 billion less in federal income taxes than we would have paid under the rates and exemptions of 1960 (not to mention the 1965 repeal of all federal excises except the liquor, tobacco, automobile, and gas taxes). At long last in 1969, the trend toward ever more generous federal income tax shelters and preferences was decisively reversed, but only at the heavy cost of tax reliefs and reductions that will exceed $8 billion by 1975.

States and localities have been doing a land-office business in taxes — especially in regressive property, excise, and sales taxes — boosting their tax collections two and a half times in this decade and raising their share of total federal-state-local tax revenues from 31% in 1960 to a projected 35½% in 1970.

Total federal, state, and local tax collections — at an estimated $310 billion in 1970 — represent nearly 32% of our Gross National Product, 4 percentage points more than in 1960. By way of comparison, when the figure was 28% for the U.S. in 1966, the ratio was 31½% in Britain and Denmark, 35% in West Germany and the Netherlands, 39% in France, and 41% in Sweden.

Taxation for Growth and Stability: A One-Way Street?

Just as the so-called "new economists" called for tax cuts to get the economy moving again during the Kennedy Administration, so they, with one voice, called for tax increases to fight inflation generated by war in Vietnam. Sad to say, when it came to tax boosts, the spirit was unwilling and the flesh was weak, with results that were a far cry from those that followed the great tax cut of 1964, of which *Business Week* said: "It isn't often that the U.S. can look back on a major change in government policy and find absolutely no grounds for criticism."[1]

Yet, the checkered course of federal tax policy in the face of the inflationary pressures generated by Vietnam in the past four years has put on the defensive those who believe in taxes as an economic regulator and, in particular, as an antidote to inflation. It is true that we expected too much of tax policy after the 1964 tax cut so dramatically delivered virtual full employment and a balanced budget by mid-1965. "Nothing exceeds like success," one critic put it. But now, we tend to expect too little. Between the bright optimism of 1965 and the black pessimism of 1970 lies a middle ground of realistic hope for the Seventies, namely, that tax adjustments can and will make a solid contribution to the objective of economic expansion without intolerable in-

---

[1] *Business Week*, February, 1965.

flation. Wherein lies that hope?

First, the tax cut of 1964 still stands tall as a testament to the force of federal tax changes in combating both inflation and recession. Indeed, it played a unique role not only in unleashing powerful expansionary forces that had been held in check by a huge fiscal over-burden, but also in serving, through its success, to clear away many of the obstacles of economic myth and misunderstanding that had for so long blocked the path to full use of the tools of modern economic policy. It is not an overstatement to say that this law ended an era in which the country felt it could afford to tolerate, or needed to tolerate, chronic unemployment and under-utilization of its resources; it also opened a new era of national commitment to the avowed and active use of tax, budget, and monetary instruments to keep the U.S. economy in a high-employment, high-growth orbit.

Second, the 1964 tax cut does not stand alone. Even before the era of the "new economics," the potency of tax policy — both good and bad — was demonstrated time and again. In the face of the Korean Conflict, Congress passed three tax bills in 1950-51 boosting taxes by an amount equivalent, in today's GNP terms, to over $35 billion (in contrast with our $12 billion surtax action in 1968). The payoff for this courageous action was a period of remarkable price stability from mid-1951 to mid-1955. In 1954, a series of tax cuts served to moderate the 1954 recession and bring it to an early end. In contrast, the failure to enact tax cuts in 1959-60 — cuts that were widely urged by economists of that day, including the timely and urgent advice from Arthur Burns to Richard Nixon early in 1960 — played an important role in letting the economy slip into the third recession of the Eisenhower Administration. Finally, although the

1968 surtax had less punch than expected, its enactment *was* followed by a leveling off of retail sales and by a steady decline in the growth rate of real GNP.

Third, one can join the chorus of critics of recent tax policy without drawing unduly gloomy inferences concerning our capacity to cope with excess demand in the future. By and large, economists came up with the correct diagnosis and advice in 1966-67; raise taxes and tighten money to stem the forces of inflation. But the prescription was not accepted soon enough by either the President or the Congress. Part of that reluctance and delay was based on a combination of anti-Vietnam sentiment plus a persistent under-estimate of the costs of that war, roadblocks that are not likely to thwart future action against inflation. Just as the success saga of the 1964 tax cut moved us a long way toward better fiscal understanding, so the bitter experience with fiscal equivocation and delay in response to Vietnam has not been lost on the thinking public. Delayed action to raise taxes was, as predicted, so costly in terms of higher prices, higher interest rates, and higher balance-of-payments deficits that I doubt that a President would ever again hesitate so long or a Congress sit idly by while inflation takes us by the throat as it did in 1966-68.

Fourth, in the fiscal wars against inflation in the future, the country has a powerful automatic weapon. Revenues from existing taxes (the surtax aside) will grow by some $15 to $17 billion a year as a built-in by-product of the growth in gross national product. That sum is the federal government's share of the nation's GNP growth of roughly $70 billion a year (in current prices). The $200 billion of federal tax revenues in 1970 (out of a GNP of about $985 billion) will grow automatically to about $280 billion by 1975 (out of a

GNP of about $1.4 trillion). It should be lot easier to exercise fiscal restraint by holding back some of this revenue bounty (i.e., not declaring "fiscal dividends" through federal program expansion or tax cuts) than it was to ram a tax increase through a reluctant Congress in 1967-68. In other words, the job of using taxes as an anti-inflationary force in the 1970's can be done for the most part (though probably not entirely) without resort to the grueling and sometimes gruesome process of wringing a tax increase out of Congress.

Fifth, with a little ingenuity and some "give" on the part of Congress, we can readily make that process less grueling, make tax policy more responsive and flexible. If we want to be able to nip recessions and inflations in the bud, we must find ways of adjusting federal tax rates more quickly and flexibly to ebbs and flows of aggregate demand. Among the promising lines of attack on this front are:[2]

  (1) Grant the President stand-by power to make temporary cuts and increases in the personal income tax, subject always to Congressional veto, along the lines of the proposals made by Presidents Kennedy and Johnson (proposals which got short shrift from a Congress jealous of its Constitutional powers of the purse).
  (2) Set up speedier Congressional procedures to respond to presidential requests for quick tax changes to head off recession or inflation, an approach that implies a "pre-

---
[2] For a further discussion of methods of increasing tax flexibility, see *Fiscal Policy for a Balanced Economy* (especially Chapter 4), a Report to the Organization for Economic Cooperation and Development (OECD) by Walter W. Heller, *et al*, December, 1968.

cooked" set of tax changes that could be swiftly activated by Congressional resolution.

(3) Develop the executive practice (suggested by Herbert Stein, now a member of the President's Council of Economic Advisers) under which the President would, as part of his budget and economic messages at the beginning of each year, routinely propose a positive *or negative* surcharge on the income tax to help stabilize the economy.

I am keenly aware of Congressional sensitivity on this subject. But Congress must also be aware of public sensitivity to inflation and recession. If President Nixon would make the call for such a speed-up in the federal tax process a bipartisan one — just as he has already put his bipartisan cachet on activist use of modern economic policy — the cause of speed and flexibility in taxation would be well-served.

Parenthetically, one should add that Congress may be a bit less reluctant to cooperate with the idea of stand-by presidential powers in this field when it considers that economic instability in the future is much more likely to take the form of occasional surges of inflation calling for tax increases rather than recessions calling for tax cuts. No one can deny that the medicine of tax increases to fight inflation tastes far more bitter than the pleasant remedy of tax cuts to fight recession and economic slack — virtue is so much easier when duty and self-interest coincide. In this light, putting the responsibility and onus of anti-inflationary tax increases on the White House might increasingly strike Congress as the better part of valor. One should also note, however, that Congressmen seem to overrate the political penalties for boosting taxes. One cannot find in the pattern of the 1968 election, for example, any evidence that a vote for the 1968 surtax was a path of political oblivion.

New National Priorities: A Call for Higher Taxes?

Timely and courageous changes in federal tax rates, as we have just seen, are an important element of an economic strategy for a "civilized economy," i.e., one that delivers high employment, lusty growth, and reasonable price stability without giving up freedom of economic choice. If we fail to stabilize the economy by available fiscal and monetary means, the next flare-up of inflation may well find the country resorting to a straight-jacket of wage and price controls — one opinion poll after another shows the American public, so devoted to freedom in general, preferring a mandatory wage and price freeze to increased taxes as a curb on spiraling prices and wages. The economist as well as the political leader will have failed in a critical job of public education as long as this mistaken preference persists, as long as the public fails to see that one of the prices of a healthy *and* free economy is willingness to bear higher taxes when the economy is over-heated.

The same economic logic that led to tax cuts in the Sixties to cope with a recession-prone economy points to higher taxes in the inflation-prone Seventies — partly in the form of foregoing further tax cuts out of that $15 to $17 billion annual revenue bounty we reap from economic growth, and partly in the form of temporary tax increases from time to time (especially if we are deter-

Seidman Lectures

mined not to endure such brutally tight money each time the economy overheats).

Going beyond economic logic, as we must, we quickly recognize that a civilized economy is hardly synonymous with a civilized society. Growth is not synonymous with progress. Ample jobs and stable prices are not synonymous with human fulfillment. Prosperity is not synonymous with the good life. Therefore, taxes enter as the price of civilization, not as a panacea, mind you — not as a sufficient condition for progress and the good life — but distinctly a necessary one.

In highlighting the quality-of-life issue in his State of the Union message and the national priority issue in his budget and economic messages, President Nixon inevitably puts before us the question of what kind of a civilization we want. How far do we want to go and how much are we willing to pay to develop the quality of our environment: to rid the physical environment of air, water, and land pollution; to rid the social environment of the cancers of poverty, ignorance, malnutrition, and disease; to rid the human environment of the urban ghetto and rural slum which blight not just the territory they occupy but the lives they oppress; to rid our personal environment of the fear of crime and violence?

Here, needless to say, we are deep in the heart of taxes. That does not mean that we should succumb to "the Washington reflex," the tendency "to discover a problem and then to throw money at it, hoping that it will somehow go away," as Senator Keating once put it. Yet, we cannot escape the cold reality that a major share of the job of cleansing our environment of pollution, of blight, of poverty, wretchedness and crime must fall on the broad fiscal shoulders of the federal government.

To be sure, one readily identifies responsibilities at the individual, industry, and state-local level. In the case of pollution, for example, the individual must exercise self-discipline, industry has to stop using the air, water, and land as dumping grounds for its waste products, and local governments are responsible for sewage disposal. The President has rightly pointed out that air and water are no longer free goods. Industry in the first instance, and ultimately the customers of industry, have to pay for the use of air and water (preferably for the cost of *not* fouling it), just as they pay for land and machinery and manpower. This is good sound economics and good sound social policy. But it will not happen without federal intervention. It has to be done by tough national regulations and penalties, regulations that treat all competitors alike, as the President has proposed.

Some implications for tax policy immediately become apparent. The object of the exercise is to stop inflicting on society the costs that the industry and its customers should legitimately bear (to "internalize the external costs," to put it in the jargon of economics). Giving special tax incentives and rewards to those who install pollution abatement facilities is the wrong road to take — it imposes the costs on the public (substituting costs in the form of tax subsidies for costs in the form of foul air and water) instead of on the users of the product, where they belong. Stiff regulations, coupled with penalties — perhaps in the form of penalty taxes — for failure to comply is the economically efficient and socially equitable approach.

But the tax implications of rescuing our physical, social and human environment go far beyond such technical tax considerations. And they far transcend the boundaries and responsibilities, and surely the fiscal capabilities, of state-local government. What we are driven back to is a question of national priorities and value preferences, and these involve the critical question of what *level of taxes* we are willing to endure as the price for improving our environment.

To make those choices intelligently calls (a) for hard numbers as to the budget room that will be available in the next few years after taking account not only of that $15-$17 billion annual revenue growth but also of the existing claims on it and (b) for a more sensible mechanism for making rational choices between public and private uses of the GNP and between civilian and defense expenditures.

With respect to the first, a series of studies in the past couple of years by Charles Schultze, George Perry, and Arthur Okun (all of the Brookings Institution) and by the Council of Economic Advisers, conclude or imply that existing claims on budget resources (including the President's proposal for revenue sharing, and the family assistance) will absorb the great bulk of the $80 billion built-in revenue growth of the next five years.

Thus, to put markedly larger resources at the disposal of programs to control our environment will require either sharp cutbacks in military outlays or increases in federal tax rates. For example, John Gardner, Chairman of the Urban Coalition, noted recently that the measures called for by the National Commission on the Causes and Prevention of Violence, chaired by Milton Eisenhower, could easily cost $20 billion a year. Noting that "we must go a good deal farther in reduction of the defense budget" and "must act to increase federal revenues," he recommended that the 5% surtax should not "under any circumstances" be allowed to lapse in mid-1970. It is not by mere chance that I cite the views of two distinguished Republicans.

Part of our problem here is that our decision-making mechanism does not make for clear-cut choices between (a) more defense and more civilian spending by government and (b) between more steaks and cars and TV sets on one hand and cleaner air and water, less crime and better schools, health, and low-income housing on the other. As long as public and private needs are not juxtaposed in a meaningful decision-making way, we will go on, by default, letting the natural distaste for higher taxes, the prejudice against them, prevail over our desire to do something about the physical, social, and human environment in which we live. Whatever may be true of public expenditures, it is clear that as to taxes, our fiscal institutions operate to accentuate the negative.

One interesting proposal to seek a more rational basis for fiscal decisions has been forwarded by Arthur Okun in his new book, *The Political Economy of Prosperity*. In effect, it would require that the $15-$17 billion annual revenue dividend be earmarked automatically for priority domestic problems, with any increase in defense programs to be matched by higher tax rates. This would mean that increases for such high-priority civilian programs as manpower training and job programs, income maintenance, health, education, urban development, and revenue sharing would not have to be financed out of left-overs from the defense program, but would compete more fairly with private expenditures. As Okum puts it:

> This procedure would change the nature of the trade-off by bringing private expenditures into the picture. Taxpayers would recognize that decisions to increase or to decrease defense spending would mean decisions to live with higher

taxes or lower them. We would reduce the intolerable pressures on our social efforts and end the absurd pitched battle between internal social welfare and external national security."[3]

One hopes that through this or other changes in our decision processes, we can make our public budget and tax decisions more rational, more expressive of our true choices. But we can never get away from the fact that in the debate over tax levels, we are deep in the realm of values. And in value judgments, it's a case of "to each his own" with no scientific, objective criteria — economic or otherwise — to guide our basic choices. I believe it is fair to say, however, that our desire, our demands for a better quality of life — for a better environment in the broad sense that I have been using here — are growing relative to our demands for a greater quantity of goods and services. Harris and Gallup polls show an increasing number of Americans not only anxious to have, but willing to pay for, this type of "good" (as opposite to "bad").

For the most part, these "goods" simply cannot be bought or delivered in the private market place. Government has to intervene to represent the parties, the public, whose interests are not represented in market transactions, in other words, to give expression to the benefits that are bestowed and costs that are inflicted upon third parties.

Partly it can do this by regulation and penalties, tax or otherwise. But for the most part, its intervention must take the form of purchasing power, cash on the barrelhead, to buy collectively those components of the

---

[3] Arthur Okun, *The Political Economy of Prosperity* (New York: W. W. Norton and Co., 1969).

better life that are desperately needed and wanted but that people will not and cannot be expected to buy individually, indeed, cannot find in the market place.

Interestingly enough, the Nixon Administration is also stressing that even for purposes of getting enough *private* expenditures into certain channels, primarily housing, we will have to accept higher federal taxes *relative* to federal expenditures, i.e., we will have to run sizable surpluses in the federal budget to make available enough private mortgage funds to do the job through the market system rather than in the form of public housing. In effect, government would be taxing away funds that would have gone into private consumption and putting them at the disposal of private investment by pumping them into private capital markets through retirement of the federal debt (or perhaps through some special institutions, like an Urban Development Bank, which would also put funds at the disposal of hard-pressed state and local governments). Here the federal government would use its vast fiscal powers to gather the funds to make them available for high-priority national uses, yet do so through private enterprise (or state-local government) rather than the federal bureaucracy. Coupling federal fiscal power with private (and state-local) initiative may not lower taxes — indeed, it may raise them — but it may also at the same time raise efficiency, lower unit costs, and lower public opposition to the payment of taxes.

Increasingly, those at or near the top of the pyramid of American society are becoming concerned, even alarmed, at the crumbling at the bottom of that pyramid as well as the physical erosion and social corrosion eating away at all levels of the structure. Repairs and improvements will be costly. The tax price of preserving and advancing civilization *is* high.

Tax Justice in an Affluent Society

Any society that calls itself civilized concerns itself deeply not just with the level of taxes but with their distribution. And affluence throws tax inequities and discrimination into ever-bolder relief. Such a civilized society demands fairness in the division of tax burdens among individuals at different income levels, i.e., vertical equity, generally identified with progressive taxation; and even-handedness in imposing taxes on people at the same income levels (adjusted for family obligations), i.e., horizontal equity or "similar taxes on those in similar circumstances." On both counts, our federal-state-local tax system falls far short of any reasonable ideal.

This subject is so vast and so much has been written on it, that I will offer no more than a few selective observations here.

In a recent article in *The Public Interest*, entitled "The Rich, the Poor, and the Taxes They Pay,"[4] Joseph Pechman has shed new light on this subject. The latest available data (for 1965) show that the federal tax system continues to be roughly proportional in the lower and middle income classes (running between 16% and 19% of income) and progressive for the higher classes (running 32% for incomes of $15,000 and over). State and local taxes are regressive throughout the income scale, dropping from 25% of income under $2,000 to 7% on incomes of $15,000 and over. Combined federal,

---

[4] Joseph A. Pechman, "The Rich, the Poor, and the Taxes They Pay," *The Public Interest*, Fall, 1969.

state, and local tax burdens (31% of income) are heaviest in the very bottom and top brackets (44% at the bottom and 38% over $15,000) and lowest in the middle brackets (27% between $2,000 and $15,000).

Pechman brings out a fourth point: While those at the bottom of the income scale receive numerous transfer payments (social security, welfare payments and the like), making them net gainers from the tax-and-transfer system, we persist in the anomaly of taxing them at the same time that we transfer income to them. This anomaly becomes all the more evident as the Congress considers the family assistance plan proposed by President Nixon. His plan amounts to a negative income tax, i.e., payments from government that are inversely correlated with poverty incomes, just as the regular income tax imposes levies that are positively correlated with livable incomes. As a part of this program, or perhaps as a prelude, we should not only remove from the income tax rolls (as, in effect, we did in the 1969 Act) families and individuals who are officially classed as poor, but follow the logic of that overdue action — which saves the poor $200 million a year — by removing the vastly larger burden — some $1.5 billion — of payroll taxes from their backs. The addition of a negative to a positive income tax clearly calls for integration of the income and payroll taxes, at least for the lowest income groups.

The widely discussed proposal for a national value-added tax (VAT) — a tax on the net addition to the value of a product at each stage of its production and distribution — also enters the vertical equity discussion. There is little doubt that the burden of the VAT would end up on the consumer and that it would be hard to prevent the VAT from shifting still further burdens onto the poor. Indeed, the VAT would further the trend, reflected in the numbers given earlier in this paper, toward reducing the relative importance of our progressive federal income tax and increasing the role of regressive payroll, property, and consumption taxes. The VAT would have to have unique, or at least decisive, advantages on other fronts — perhaps as an instrument of economic stabilization, perhaps on the balance-of-payments front (though separate border taxes, also distasteful, could do this job as well without having the tail wag the dog), perhaps as a last-resort source of additional revenue — to be acceptable. I do not discern such advantages.

When we turn to special income tax shelters, privileges, and preferences — notice that I do not use the loaded word "loopholes," the word that even Justice Brandeis avoided when he described a particularly glaring tax preference as "a plain, unvarnished bonanza of a windfall" — we are in an area where vertical and horizontal equity interlock. For on the basis of his studies, Pechman concludes that far from paying anything like the statutory rate of 70% in the top bracket,

> "after allowing for all the subtractions permitted by the tax laws — many of them perfectly appropriate, but others nothing less than outright tax handouts — the maximum average rate for even the highest income classes is no more than about 30% on reported income and 20% on total income (i.e., income that is not taxed and not reported on tax returns). By any test of equity, the Federal income tax leaves much to be desired — although I hasten to add that, despite its

faults, this tax is still the best in the nation's revenue system."[5]

Both to narrow the gap between the apparent and real progressivity in the federal income tax and to reduce the grossly unequal treatment among people in equal income and family circumstances, the tax reform movement must be vigorously pursued. Leaving aside the high price paid in tax relief for the reforms of the 1969 Act — the $8 billion-plus price tag by 1975 is vastly excessive in the face of our unfilled and aching social needs — we can still applaud the significant and pathbreaking inroads into special tax shelters for real estate, capital gains, the oil and gas industry, farm hobby losses, and the like, as well as the establishment of the minimum income tax principle. But now that the path is at least blazed, it is important to use it, to press forward with further action along the following lines:

(1) Narrow the tax privileges for the oil and mining industries, especially through the elimination of double deductions for intangible drilling and development costs and further cutbacks in their depletion and capital gains shelters;

(2) Tighten the tax on capital gains still further, especially by removing the wide-open escape hatch of non-realization of capital gains at death;

(3) Change the federal subsidy for state-local borrowing from a tax exemption (much of whose benefit goes to wealthy taxpayers

---
[5] Joseph A. Pechman, "Tax Policies for the 1970's," *Public Policy*, Fall, 1969, p. 87.

Seidman Lectures

rather than desperate state and local governments) to some form of direct federal sharing of state-local bond interest payments;
(4) Re-examine the entire system of deductions for the elderly and for contributions, interests, and taxes to make sure that those that cannot be justified as the best method of serving some important social purpose — for surely, most of them cannot be justified on the basis of tax theory — be narrowed or eliminated.

This is admittedly a tough and rigorous approach to the subject of tax shelters. But it must be pressed, year-in, year-out, on a bunker-by-bunker and foxhole-by-foxhole basis if necessary. For these tax preferences are now costing the federal budget huge sums, sums that are in substance just as much of a charge on that budget as the outlays that are officially labeled "expenditures." Reduced income is algebraically the same as increased outgo. A recent exhaustive analysis by the U.S. Treasury showed that tax preferences — in effect, "tax expenditures" that are alternatives to direct government expenditures or government lending programs — were extending huge benefits to various groups. For example, in 1968, these included:

(1) $1.6 billion to the resource industries, especially oil and gas (through expensing of certain capital costs, percentage depletion in excess of cost depletion, and special capital gains treatment for iron ore and coal royalties).
(2) $1.0 billion in the field of agriculture and agriculture resources, primarily through ex-

penses and capital gains treatment.
(3) $4.0 billion for community development and housing, mostly through deductibility of mortgage interest and property taxes, but partly through excess depreciation on rental housing.
(4) $2.3 billion to the elderly, part of a vast sum of $15.6 billion for health and welfare, through such provisions as additional exemptions and credits, exclusion of employee pensions, deductibility of charitable contributions, and the standard deduction.

The case for reviewing and tightening these provisions does not rest only on equity grounds. Economic efficiency loudly calls for removing unwanted tax interference with the free and efficient flow of resources. I say "unwanted" because the nation obviously believes that in at least a few special instances the tax mechanism ought to be used to stimulate resource flow into certain uses, i.e., believes that tax subsidies should be paid to divert the flow of resources into the favored pursuits at the cost of higher taxes on the non-favored ones. But believers in the efficiency of the market system should always keep in mind that it is a diversion and a distortion. To the extent that the pre-tax pattern of profits is the best guide to the allocation of resources into alternative uses, the post-tax allocation under our system of myriad special privileges involves a substantial cost in loss of efficiency, loss of output, and higher costs.

These considerations should also be borne in mind in considering the case for tax credits as a means of accomplishing social objectives rather than doing it through direct government subsidies. It is devilishly difficult to focus a tax credit sharply enough so that it will go only to those who do the desired things, say, build low-income housing or set up businesses in the ghetto; who would not have done them otherwise; and who will not be able to convert the tax credit into a tax loophole by actions that qualify it for the tax benefit in appearance but not in substance. As Stanley Surrey once put it, special tax incentives for ghetto reconstruction and the like are prone to become tax bonanzas that might make "tax millionaires out of doctors, lawyers, and other investors." It is easier to control federal subsidies and make them efficient if they are open and aboveboard as part of the expenditure budget.

The road to tax equity and even-handed treatment of different resource uses is a long and hard one. But it is a road that a society that wants to call itself civilized must travel.

Strengthening Our Fiscal Federalism

President Nixon's proposal for revenue sharing recognizes another essential in the battle for a better balanced society and a stronger federalism. Sustained prosperity has highlighted as never before the fiscal imbalance between federal and state-local governments, the fiscal mismatch that arises because growth bestows its revenue bounties on the federal government (chiefly through the progressive income tax) while imposing the major part of its burdens on state and local governments. How we resolve that imbalance — whether it be through tax sharing, increased federal aids, perhaps credits against the federal income tax for state income tax payments — will have a major impact on: the harshness of the terms on which state and local government strike a balance between their rapidly rising expenditure obligations and their limited — and often over-worked — tax base; the shape of our federal fiscal system, both as to the overall distribution of our federal-state-local tax burdens and the geographical inequalities in tax burdens and service levels; and the relative strength of federal and state-local governments, or to put it differently, the basic role and vitality of the states in our federal system.

When the state-local taxpayer is beset with — indeed, rebelling against — a rising tide of regressive and repressive property, sales, and excise taxes, it makes little sense to weaken or dismantle the progressive and growth-responsive federal income tax. Whether our concern is for efficiency in taxation, better balance in our federalism, or a more rational system of financing our pressing social needs, there is no escape from the logic of putting the power of the federal income tax at the disposal of beleaguered state and local governments.

The essence of tax sharing — in the form previously known as the "Heller-Pechman plan," but now that the President has adopted and espoused most of it, more properly known as the "Heller-Pechman-Nixon plan!" — is as follows:

(1) The federal government would regularly distribute to the state and local governments a certain percentage of the federal income tax base (the amount reported as net taxable income by all individuals — 2% under the "Heller-Pechman plan" and an eventual 1% under the Nixon plan).

(2) The basic distribution would be on a straight population formula, so-and-so-much per capita, with adjustments for tax effort under

both plans, so that states taxing themselves more heavily than the national average would get more, and those exerting less tax effort would get less of the federal tax shares; greater inter-state equalization, under the Heller-Pechman plan, by setting aside 10% of the proceeds for distribution to the 17 poorest states.
(3) Both plans call for a mandatory pass-through to local units, with special weight given to the plight of the urban areas in the intrastate allocation formula (a point on which the Nixon plan needs strengthening).
(4) The widest possible discretion ("no strings attached") would be given state and local governments in the use of the funds, subject only to the usual accounting and auditing requirements, compliance with the Civil Rights Act (a proviso conspicuously missing from the Nixon proposal), and perhaps a ban on the use of such funds for highways (which already have a special federal trust fund used for their benefit).

Why is the case for federal tax sharing so compelling? Let me give a brief six-fold answer:
(1) First, it would significantly relieve the immediate pressures on state-local treasuries, and, more important, make state-local revenues more responsive to economic growth. Had the plan been in effect in 1955, the distribution of 2% of the $125 billion income tax base in that year would have yielded a state-local tax share of about $2½

billion; by 1972, the base should be about $425 billion, which would yield an $8½ billion annual share.
(2) Second, tax sharing would serve our federalist interest in state-local vitality and independence by providing new financial elbow room, free of political penalty, for creative state and local officials.
(3) Third, tax sharing would help reverse the present regressive trend in our federal-state-local tax system.
(4) Fourth, tax sharing — especially with the 10% equalization feature — would enable the economically weaker states to upgrade the scope and quality of their services without putting crushingly heavier burdens on their citizens.
(5) Fifth, the plan would incorporate a stimulus to state and local tax efforts. If it were supplimented by a federal income tax credit, this stimulus would be even greater.
(6) Finally, it would relieve some of the intense fiscal pressures on local, and particularly urban, governments. On the understanding that tax sharing would not be substituted for federal aids, but be a supplement thereto, it would bring significant support for the general local enterprise, not just the specific services that are supported by federal aid as being directly in the national interest. It is hard to argue that sanitation, green space, recreation, police and fire protection, street maintenance and lighting, have large spillover effects on other communities. Hence,

they do not qualify under our present system of federal grants-in-aid. Yet, in more or less humdrum services like these lies much of the difference between a decent and a squalid environment, between a snug suburb and a grinding ghetto, in short, between a less and a more civilized community.

Conclusion

We enter the 1970's sobered, not so much by the burdens of taxation we must bear, as by the burdens that taxation, especially federal taxation, must bear. Consider once again the demands we make on the federal tax system:

(1) To fight inflation both in its endemic form and in its occasional epidemic form;

(2) To finance the federal government's large share of the vast job of completing what one observer called "our half-finished society," of converting growth into progress, prosperity into the good life, jobs and income into fulfillment;

(3) To strike a more equitable and more efficient balance between taxes on the upper and lower income groups and between those who now escape and those who already pay their appropriate share of the tax burden;

(4) Finally, to relieve state-local government of the fiscal strings that tend to enfeeble such governments and, hence, to undermine our fiscal federalism.

The job that lies ahead is truly a national responsibility in the sense that every segment of the population and every level of government must participate in it. As I said in the Godkin Lectures in 1966, "the good life will not come, ready-made, from some federal assembly-line. It has to be custom-built, engaging the effort and imagination and resourcefulness of the community." I might have added, "and the willingness of our citizens to bear the cost in higher taxes that are the price for a more civilized society."

"The Role of Taxation in Meeting Social Problems"

Lecture Two

by Paul R. McDaniel

As the urgency to meet our nation's pressing social problems mounts, it is perhaps not surprising that proposals to utilize the tax system as a means of funding the various responsive efforts proliferate. The effort to reform our Federal income tax system that culminated in the Tax Reform Act of 1969 shed considerable light on the possibilities and limitations inherent in the use of the tax system as a tool in meeting social needs. Proposals to use the tax system to meet nontax objectives must be evaluated by citizens in their dual roles as taxpayers and as citizens concerned to provide the quality of life that is the birthright of all Americans. An informed judgment thus requires an understanding of the impact on the tax system — and hence on all taxpayers — of the use of tax measures to meet social problems.

The great cost of dealing with pollution, unemployment, education, housing, health care and the like have led many concerned individuals and political leaders to examine and propose the use of what are generally referred to by their proponents as "tax incentives." Consideration of the merits of these proposals is better undertaken in terms of a somewhat different concept, however, that of "tax expenditures." The phrase "tax incentives" tends to beg one of the significant questions to be answered in any Federally financed project that requires cooperation of the private sector: will persons in private enterprise in fact be motivated to address themselves to a given problem, such as pollution, if Federal funds are made available? Utilization of the concept of "tax incentives" tends to imply an affirmative answer to this critical question by definition. Further, some theorists posit the Federal income tax as a disincentive, so that selective modification of the tax burden for a given purpose would merely constitute removal of this disincentive effect, not a positive incentive.

In this discussion, then it will be more helpful to refer to the neutral, and more descriptive, term "tax expenditures." After outlining the "tax expenditure" concept and the impact of tax expenditures in general on the Federal income tax system, we will analyze the implications of the use of tax expenditures to solve three social problems: education, pollution, and housing.

The Analytical Framework of the Tax Expenditure Concept

Tax expenditures may take the form of tax deductions, tax credits, deferrals of tax, preferential rates or exemptions from tax. Many of the deductions in the tax code arose out of a conscious effort to encourage a particular type of activity. The deduction for charitable contributions appears to be such a provision. On the

Seidman Lectures

other hand, many of the present tax preferences have arisen more by accident than by design, frequently because policymakers or administrators did not fully recognize the implications of their actions. The deduction for percentage depletion and preferential tax rules for farmers are examples of this kind of special tax benefit. Interestingly, these tax preferences are now defended by their beneficiaries as needed incentives for the particular economic activity affected.

The adverse effects of these tax preferences on the equity of the Federal income tax system have long been recognized and denounced by tax theorists. But another consequence has only recently been recognized and brought to public attention. That is, that these tax preferences in fact constitute public expenditures just as much as direct expenditures of Federal funds that result from the normal Congressional appropriations process.

This analysis was articulated by former Secretary of the Treasury Joseph Barr in testimony before the Joint Economic Committee in January 1969 and in the 1968 Annual Report of the Secretary of the Treasury. Simply stated, the Treasury thesis was that a tax preference item can be viewed as if the Internal Revenue Service had collected the tax from the taxpayer claiming the tax benefit and then Congress had appropriated the funds for payment in the amount of the tax preference for the purpose specified.

As an example, the deduction for interest paid on home mortgages is generally defended as an incentive to encourage home ownership. But note how this tax benefit looks when viewed as a tax expenditure. The tax rule in effect says that if a married couple has more than $200,000 of income, then for each $100 of interest liability that is incurred on their home mortgage, the federal government will pay $70 to the savings and loan association on the homeowner's account, while the homeowner will put up $30. This result, of course, merely reflects the after-tax impact of the interest deduction for a 70 percent bracket taxpayer. But for the taxpayer in the 20 percent bracket, present tax expenditure policy provides that the homeowner must pay the lending institution $80 in interest in order to obtain a $20 matching grant from the Federal government. And if a very low income person who does not earn enough to enter the tax rolls buys a house, the Federal government will not contribute anything through the tax expenditure mechanism to assist in his interest payments.

The question that tax expenditure analysis confronts the policymaker with, then, is whether the result described represents a rational approach to encourage home ownership by our citizens. More pointedly, would Congress enact a system that provided for direct payment of the Government's share of the interest expense in the proportions that result under our present tax rules?

Other tax preferences can be similarly recast as tax expenditures. Thus, the percentage depletion allowance can be viewed as a tax expenditure to encourage drilling activity; the preferential rate for capital gains as a subsidy for entrepreneurial business activity; or the medical expense deduction as a Federal program to share medical costs. The mode of Federal participation in a particular transaction through tax expenditures may vary depending on the form in which the tax benefit is cast. In some cases, the Federal contribution may resemble a low cost loan program, in others an interest subsidy, in others a direct or matching grant system. But a tax expenditure may always be recast in the form of a direct nontax financial benefit conferred by the government.

Identifying the Tax Expenditure

If the foregoing describes the operation of a tax expenditure, the question then is, how does one identify a tax expenditure? To put the question another way, by what criteria do we establish that a particular provision in the tax laws constitutes a tax expenditure rather than an integral part of the tax structure?

One fundamental judgment must be accepted to establish the criteria: A tax system has an internal logic that results from the values society has determined inherent in a fair tax system. Society may employ different values in choosing the variety of tax systems under which we operate. Thus, the Federal individual income tax system expresses society's judgment that this fundamental tax should be progressive; the more income one receives, the higher rate of tax he should pay on his last dollar of income. A different value judgment underlies sales taxes, however, which bear on all persons in proportion to their taxable purchases regardless of income. The point for our analysis is that certain criteria can be articulated which will differentiate provisions that merely involve a working out of the implications of society's judgments about the nature of the tax system from provisions that in fact are antithetical to the fundamental precept of the particular tax system.

Within the context of the Federal income tax system, I would propose that the following criteria can be used to identify tax expenditures:

(1) Any item determined to be income that is exempt from tax constitutes a tax expenditure.

(2) Any item that reduces progressivity is a tax expenditure.
(3) Any item that can be restated as a program of direct financial assistance without violating the precepts of a progressive income tax system is a tax expenditure.

These three principles overlap, but each deals with a somewhat different problem. The first criterion deals with the question of exemptions from tax. In the Federal income tax system, society has chosen to tax "income." Thus variations in the tax load resulting from determinations of what kinds of receipts are treated as income do not constitute tax expenditures. A determination by Congress or the courts that a given receipt of money or property constitutes, e.g. a return of capital, and not income, does no violence to the internal logic of an income tax system. Hence, the rule that a recovery of taxes previously paid does not constitute income is entirely consistent with the logic of an income tax system and exclusion of such an item from tax will do no violence to progressivity, since this conclusion is consistent with an economic view that there has been no net accretion in wealth that would justify treating the item as income.

On the other hand, once an item is determined to be income, i.e. a net accretion in wealth, such as interest on state and local bonds, then exemption from tax violates the logical demands of an income tax system. Exemption of state and local bond interest from tax thus would constitute a tax expenditure under any income tax system whether progressive or proportional.

The second criteria is that any provision in the Federal income tax laws that reduces progressivity constitutes a tax expenditure. This principle would also apply to tax exemption once the definition hurdle is cleared, but is most useful in analyzing deductions and deferrals of tax. At the outset we can put aside the question of business deductions and deductions related to the cost of producing income. The internal logic of a tax on net income dictates that these deductions do not adversely affect progressivity, but rather flow from society's judgment that the tax is imposed on net income. This second criteria focuses attention on three types of tax provisions: one, personal deductions, such as charitable contributions; two, tax provisions that alter the timing of deductions so as to permit a mismatching of income and the expenses of producing that income, as for example accelerated depreciation of real estate; and three, deductions in amounts that exceed the cost of producing income, such as percentage depletion.

All such provisions do violence to the fundamental precepts of a progressive income tax system. That is, these provisions permit two taxpayers with the same amount of economic income to pay the same or a lower amount of tax than another taxpayer with less income. Hence, all such deductions may be viewed as tax expenditures.

The third criteria I suggest is that a tax expenditure is any item that can be restated in terms of a direct government program of financial assistance, *without violating the progressivity concept*. This principle is needed to account for rate differentials in a tax system. One can ask, if an exemption of an income item constitutes a tax expenditure, does not a rate differential also constitute a tax expenditure to the person who pays at the lower rate? For example, assume two individuals, one with an effective rate of 50 percent and other of 20 percent.

Would tax expenditure analysis assert that the 20 percent rate can be viewed as if the government had collected tax at a 50 percent rate and made a direct grant back to the lower income individual of the taxes represented by the 30 percent differential? The answer to this question is negative, because as so restated the direct expenditure assumes a principle that is directly antithetical to a progressive tax system, i.e. it assumes a proportional income tax system that utilizes a 50 percent rate. Thus, under the proposed criteria, the rate differentials in a progressive tax system do not constitute tax expenditures.

But what of the personal exemption? The common analysis asserts that a personal exemption constitutes simply a dollar amount of income that is taxed at a zero rate. So viewed a basic personal exemption is not a tax expenditure, since taxing a given amount of income at a zero rate is no more regressive than taxing it at 1 percent or 14 percent. This point would be patently clear if the tax system employed negative rates.

On the other hand, the additional exemption for the elderly and the blind does constitute a tax expenditure. These exemptions are awarded on a factor unrelated to income, namely age or physical condition, and thus violate both the logical integrity of an income tax system and the principle of progressivity. The personal exemption in present law can be viewed as containing a partial tax expenditure element to the extent the amount varies with family size. While it is logically defensible to tax a given amount of income at a zero rate, the size of that income bracket should not vary on account of factors unrelated to income, namely the size of the family.

Arguments Against Tax Expenditures

The fundamental argument against tax expenditures from the standpoint of tax theorists is that each tax preference reduces the fairness of the tax system. No tax expenditure has yet been proposed that avoids this criticism. The tax preferences in the present system, and those that have been proposed, either provide a greater benefit to those in the seventy percent bracket than to those in the twenty percent bracket, or permit different taxpayers with the same income to bear a dissimilar tax burden on account of factors totally extraneous to the production of income. And no tax incentive provides any benefit to a person who is not on the tax rolls.

The major defects cited by opponents of tax expenditures are now well-known, and will only be listed here. The weight of these objections can be better evaluated in the context of the particular tax provisions discussed below. Tax expenditures constitute, as Chairman Wilbur Mills has put it, "backdoor" spending. That is, these expenditures are insulated from annual Congressional review in the appropriations process. This form of Federal expenditure thus tends to remain imbedded in our economic structure long after its usefulness or desirability has ceased. Tax expenditures are inefficient to the extent that they reward taxpayers for engaging in a course of conduct they would have followed in any event. In addition, funds may be expended in low rather than high priority areas, since there is generally no control over allocation of funds.

Tax expenditures, it is also argued, result in a misallocation of resources, both public and private. In the private sector, tax incentives encourage capital to be utilized in a manner that will maximize the tax benefit.

But the resulting allocation of capital may not be directed to the most efficient or even the most desirable solutions to the problem addressed. In short, the existence of tax preferences distorts the normal businessman's decision making process. From a national standpoint, since tax expenditures are not subject to the appropriations process, tax expenditures automatically assume a role of first priority for our national expenditures in an amount determined solely by the beneficiaries of each preference. The Treasury 1968 Study mentioned earlier identified some $40 billion in annual tax expenditures. This is a very substantial amount of Federal funds to expend each year without any Congressional review, especially when these expenditures result in other taxpayers paying high rates of tax to provide revenues needed for direct Federally assisted programs.

Arguments for Tax Expenditures

To list the arguments against expenditures through tax preferences is in a sense to set forth the arguments in favor of the use of tax incentives. For example, in answer to those who assert that tax expenditures are not reviewed by Congress, proponents of tax expenditures argue that one of the benefits is that taxpayers can plan their affairs with the certainty that the rules of the game will not be quickly changed, nor will the level of funding ride the appropriations roller coaster that marks so many Federal programs.

Similarly, it is argued that Federal expenditures through tax incentives leave room for private initiative and decision making, free of bureaucratic constraints and lack of imagination. Tax incentives, so viewed, represent a commitment to private enterprise in our economic system, and, if properly structured, need lose little in terms of efficiency or effectiveness. For it certainly cannot be maintained that inefficiency and diluted effort are absent from directly funded and Federally administered programs.

Proponents also argue that tax incentives are simple and do not involve the red tape that is the hallmark of Federal programs. Finally, and of direct interest to our present discussion, tax incentives can involve private business and individuals in the solution of our social problems.

Toward a Resolution of the Conflict

Our analysis of the nature of tax expenditures and the arguments for and against their use permit certain conclusions:

(1) Any tax expenditure can be translated to and effected by a direct expenditure of appropriated funds and still satisfy the asserted advantages of a tax preference. For example, a direct Federal grant, or loan program can be drafted and operated as simply, and with the same degree of freedom from government control as a tax expenditure, if these are determined to be the overriding criteria for the program.

(2) With one exception, any direct expenditure method can be drafted as a tax expenditure program in such a way as to avoid the disadvantages that opponents of tax incentive cite. For example, a one year termination date can be placed on tax expenditures to incur annual Congressional review in the

light of budgetary needs and priority controls.
(3) It is thus clear that an argument for tax incentives is not really an argument for any inherent advantages of Federal spending through the tax system. It is in fact an argument in favor of Federal spending for specific purposes as opposed to less or no Federal spending for those purposes. The asserted advantages of tax incentives are quite independent of the tax system and can be as easily realized in a direct expenditure program.
(4) The only difference between tax expenditures and direct expenditures is that the use of tax incentives will impair the fairness of the income tax system.

If these conclusions are valid, then the conflict between the two positions can be seen in more fundamental terms. Those who oppose use of the tax system to meet social or economic problems do so, not because they oppose expenditure of Federal funds for the desired purpose, but because they do not want to see the funds expended in a manner that will impinge on one of the fundamental values of our society — a fair tax system.

Proponents of tax incentives, on the other hand, feel that the social need of the proposed object of the Federal expenditures overrides the value to society of a fair system in the particular area of their concern. It is so important that funds be expended for the prescribed purpose that any means of securing the funds must be adopted. But as social needs multiply, these demands in the aggregate can undermine society's value judgment that a progressive tax system is the fair and proper measure of each citizen's contribution to government.

Thus, the strategy for those who desire to maintain the integrity and purpose of a progressive income tax system is becoming increasingly clear. To prevent the use of or to effect the removal of tax preferences in order to attain a fair tax system, tax reformers must not only point up the deleterious effects of tax incentives, but also must point the way to a solution of the social need giving rise to the demand for tax expenditures. This requires that the tax purist be able to identify and quantify the contours of the demand being made in each area of social need, and suggest alternatives which will satisfy these desiderata while preserving a fair income tax system.

It is helpful to turn to an examination of tax incentives in three areas of social need — education, pollution, and housing — and analyze the impact of those provisions in light of the tax expenditure concept. For if our analysis is correct thus far, this discussion should point the way to alternative solutions that will meet the dual moral imperative: a fair tax system and Federal financial assistance to these specific social problems.

Tax Expenditures For Education

Present income tax laws provide Federal financial assistance to education at several different levels. A charitable contribution deduction is granted to individuals who contribute to educational institutions. Tax exemption is accorded to qualifying educational organizations. A personal exemption is accorded to the parents of a student even though he is over age 18 and has some income of his own. The student himself can exclude scholarship funds from income.

During consideration of the Tax Reform Act of 1969, a good deal of attention focused on the operation of the charitable contribution deduction, especially with respect to gifts of appreciated property.

The charitable contribution deduction clearly constitutes a tax expenditure. A $100 cash gift by an individual in the seventy percent bracket to his college is equivalent to an expenditure by the Federal government of $70, with a net cost to the donor of $30. But if a twenty-five percent bracket taxpayer gives $100 in cash to the same college, the government will only bear $25 of the cost of this gift. And an individual who does not itemize his deductions may be assuming the full burden of his $100 gift.

If one views this system as a matching Federal grant system, its inherent irrationality is striking. A direct grant statute modeled on present tax rules would provide that the Federal government will match the gift of married individuals who have more than $200,000 of income on the basis of $7 for each $3 they contribute to charity. For those with $52,000 of income, the al matching formula is $5 for each $5 donated. If the donor's income is $16,000, for each $7.50 given, the Government will pay $2.50 to the charitable recipient.

If this direct matching system were presented to Congress as the proper incentive for charitable giving, it is safe to predict that it would receive short shrift. Yet this is precisely the effect of the present expenditure mechanism embodied in Federal income tax laws.

The impact of this system on the tax laws is directly inverse to the theory of a progressive tax system. For the underlying rationale of present rules is that the more money a person has with which to make charitable gifts, the less it costs him to make the gift. Conversely, the less money he has with which to make charitable gifts, the more out-of-pocket expense he must absorb.

The situation is aggravated when gifts are made in the form of appreciated property. In this transaction, not only is a deduction granted for the full fair market value of the property, but the income represented by the gain is not subject to tax. This combination of exemption of income plus full deduction produces even more peculiar contours as an expenditure policy. For the 70 percent bracket donor, making a gift of property worth $100 with a basis of zero, the Government grants a $70 tax reduction via the deduction plus $35 in the form of forgiven capital gains tax. A corresponding direct expenditure system would be broken down as follows: if a married donor with more than $200,000 of income makes a gift of $30 to charity, the Government will make a grant to the charity of $70 and return his $35 of tax to the donor. In other words, the Government will pay $105 to encourage a $100 gift to charity, if the donor is in the highest tax bracket. On the other hand, a married donor with $52,000 of income wishing to benefit his college in the amount of $100, would have to make a gift of $50 to charity, which the government would match with $50, and would return only $25 to the donor. In this case, it costs the Government only $75 to induce the $100 charitable donation.

This analysis not only points to the unfairness inherent in the tax rules governing charitable gifts of appreciated property, but also delineates the unequal treatment given to gifts of cash, even though the dollar benefit charity receives is identical. The difference in treatment in terms of a direct expenditure analysis is that the donor of appreciated property pays no tax on the income from which the gift is paid, whereas the donor of cash makes his gift out of after-tax income.

Tax expenditure analysis thus demonstrates the irrationality and unfairness of the present system of providing tax incentives to education through the charitable contribution deduction. Why then do we continue such a system? The answer is to be found in the testimony of the colleges and universities, and some wealthy donors, before the Senate Finance Committee in connection with proposed changes in the Tax Reform Act affecting the charitable contribution deduction.

Colleges and universities presented a highly organized front in the hearings before the Senate Finance Committee. Their position can be simply stated. Education is of critical importance to the social, economic and political progress of the United States; institutions of higher learning must have ever increasing funds to meet educational needs; the charitable contribution deduction helps provide funds; therefore, colleges and universities oppose any change in that tax provisions that might result in reduced amounts being donated to them by private individuals.

Attention in the Senate primarily was concentrated on proposed changes in the treatment of gifts of appreciated property and on indirect methods of limiting the benefits of the charitable contribution deduction provision, such as through the minimum tax proposal.

Colleges and universities made two basic arguments to support their contention that changes in the rules for the charitable contribution deduction would impair their financial condition:

(1) The tax deduction generally, and the special treatment for gifts of appreciated property

Seidman Lectures

in particular, constitute incentives to charitable giving. Any diminution in the tax incentive will correspondingly reduce funds available for education.

(2) Private support of education is important in a pluralistic society and the tax laws should encourage participation by the private sector. sector.

It is important to evaluate these arguments since they point up the dimensions that a more rational national tax policy must assume.

In 1967 individuals claimed charitable contribution deductions of over $9 billion. Of this amount, 92 percent was given in the form of cash and only 8 percent in the form of property. These figures reflect only gifts by persons who itemize their deductions; additional gifts by persons claiming the standard deduction are estimated to be around $4 billion.

Quantification of the disincentive argument advanced by charities is difficult. It is plain that the tax laws provide no incentive for giving by nonitemizers. It is reasonable to expect that their charitable gifts would remain the same regardless of changes in the deduction. Some studies have also indicated that nontax considerations primarily motivate donors who itemize in income tax brackets below 40 percent.

Thus, the disincentive argument of the colleges and universities would appear to be confined largely to taxpayers in the above 40 percent brackets, and the special treatment accorded gifts of appreciated property. Less than 1.5 million taxpayers out of over 27 million contributors fall in these high income brackets but they contribute about one-fourth of the $9 billion in itemized charitable contributions and almost two-thirds of the gifts of appreciated property.

Colleges and universities argue that they would be seriously affected by any changes because they are especially reliant on large gifts by wealthy donors and on gifts of appreciated property.

The present difficulty is that there is no reliable quantification of the disincentive effect on these donors of changes in the tax rules. Would charitable contributions be reduced by $1 for each $1 of additional taxes that were required to be paid, or by one-half or one-fourth of the additional taxes? No one really knows. Presumably there is a role for systems analysis in this situation to provide some insight as to the probable effects of any proposed changes.

What is significant for the present discussion is that this possibility of reduced giving to colleges and universities must be taken into account as one parameter of any proposed new system of encouraging charitable giving.

The second tenet of the colleges and universities is that private philanthropy must be encouraged through the tax system to insure pluralism in our total educational effort. But the American Council on Education testified that only one percent of donors gave seventy-five percent of the gifts to higher education in 1962-63. Since these gifts obviously come from the wealthiest members of our society, from the standpoint of tax reformers it appeared that the tax preferences involved in the charitable deduction rules are a very high price to pay for a very minimal amount of pluralism. Nonetheless, any proposal for change must reflect the underlying concern that private individuals need to be involved in and have the right to select the objects of their philanthropy.

Seidman Lectures 45

In sum, opponents of tax expenditures through the charitable contribution deduction argue that the present system is defective on several counts. For the vast majority of givers, the deduction is simply a windfall which pays them to make gifts they would make in any event. In some cases, the cost of the gift to the government is greater than the amount charity receives. As such, the Federal expenditure is inefficient and wasteful. The present tax rules are inequitable, giving a larger benefit to the wealthy than to lower income taxpayers and a marked preference for those who can make their charitable gifts by using appreciated property as compared to those who must use cash.

Proponents of present tax incentives for charitable giving essentially are concerned that badly needed sources of revenue for education will dry up with removal of the tax preferences. They want to encourage private involvement in education and to be free of the vagaries of Government control and the annual appropriations process.

In the consideration of the Tax Reform Bill these two positions passed without making constructive contact. Tax reformers reacted adversely to the general refusal of charities to consider seriously the inequities inherent in present tax rules. On the other hand, colleges and universities seemed generally to conclude that insistence on removal of tax preferences implied a lack of concern for education.

Nonetheless out of the debate there emerges the contours of a viable new system that can satisfy the legitimate concerns of each of these positions. From the standpoint of tax equity, the answer is that the deduction for charitable contributions must be eliminated, and that transfers of appreciated property will constitute taxable transactions.

But as suggested above, advancement of this proposition imposed the responsibility on reformers to propose an alternative means of funding education's needs. It was the failure to provide such an alternative that led to the defeat of many of the admittedly limited reforms advocated for the Tax Reform Bill. But the testimony of colleges and universities of philanthropists suggests at least the conditions that must be met by such an alternative:

(1) Educational institutions must be assured that present and projected levels of support equal that which they can reasonably anticipate from the present tax expenditure system.
(2) The process must be free of Federal control.
(3) Private donors must have a voice in determining the recipients of charitable support.

These criteria can be met without impairing the equity of the tax system. The proposal suggested for consideration is that we shift to a direct Federal matching grant system. That is, a formula would be employed by which the Federal government would automatically match all or a portion of a contributor's gift to charity. The proper index for the formula would appear to be the proportion of a taxpayer's total economic income that he gives to charity.

For example, the new system could provide that if a person gives thirty percent of his total income to charity, the Treasury will match his gift dollar for dollar. The taxpayer who gives fifteen percent of his income to charity would have one-half of his gift matched by the Treasury, and so on. Detailed analysis would be required to determine the exact formula needed to provide funds

Seidman Lectures

to charity of the magnitude required and at a level consistent with projected Federal revenue needs.

Such a system would introduce equity into our Federal system for encouraging charitable giving. For, under the proposal, the low income individual who gives a large share of his income to charity will have his gift matched on the same basis as a wealthy individual who gives the same percentage of his income to charity. As noted above, that is not the result under the present tax incentive system.

The proposal, of course, means that charitable institutions receiving gifts from the vast majority of givers who are not tax motivated will benefit more from these gifts than they do at the present time. There is no reason to expect that changes in the tax rules will result in a significant reduction in the level of giving by these individuals.

On the other hand, educational institutions may derive somewhat less benefit from gifts by wealthy individuals. For example, a $100 gift by a seventy percent taxpayer now costs him only $30. If we assume that he will reduce his gift with the removal of the tax benefit to his present $30 cost, his college could only get a maximum of $60 if a dollar for dollar matching system were adopted as the upper limit of the Treasury contribution. To get the same $100 to his college, this taxpayer would have to increase the out-of-pocket cost of his gift at least to $50.

To preserve individual choice and involvement, each donor would be entitled to designate on his tax return the organizations that are to receive the matching gifts triggered by his donations. The donor could also designate the amounts that each designated institution is to receive.

A permanent appropriation could be provided for the Federal matching funds triggered by the formula. This would provide certainty to charities and freedom from problems of the annual appropriations process.

A liberal period of time would be required for transition to the new system to insure stable levels of receipts for charitable organizations. In addition, during the transition period, one deviation from equity might be considered to ease the problems of institutions of higher education that rely heavily on large gifts. The top matching formula might be triggered by any gift in excess of a substantial minimum amount, regardless of the percentage of the donor's income that the gift represented.

The proposed system would facilitate consideration of relative priorities that society might wish to place on various charitable activities. If education is of first priority, then a higher matching formula could be provided for it than for a lower priority charitable activity. The present tax system accomplishes this result in a rough fashion by placing differing limits on deductible contributions; but the direct matching system would enable Congress to make more sophisticated judgments.

This proposal seems to satisfy the requirements of tax reformers and educational institutions alike. Further analysis is, of course, required. But, the attempt here is simply to provide a framework within which those concerned with two vital social needs can cooperatively achieve their respective goals — tax equity and funds to meet our pressing education requirements.

A final note should be added. Federal incentives for charitable giving, recast in this mold, present rather interesting implications for the role of private foundations. If private foundations were to continue to qualify as charitable recipients, Congress would be squarely faced with the implications of the following pattern. A wealthy donor could create a private foundation. Upon making a gift to the foundation, he would trigger a matching grant by the Federal Government to his foundation. The Federal portion would then be fully controlled by the trustees of the foundation from that time forth. They would only be required to meet the income payout and other foundation rules passed by Congress. It is interesting to speculate whether Congress would acquiesce in a system that permanently placed Federal funds in the hands of a foundation created by the donor and insulated those monies from publicly determined priorities. But, of course, as Senator Albert Gore pointed out in his proposal to limit the tax exempt life of foundations to forty years, this is precisely the system we now have via the tax expenditure mechanism. The direct matching proposal at least permits Congress to face squarely the implications of channeling charitable contributions through private foundations.

Tax Expenditures and Problems of Pollution

With the quality of the environment occupying stage center of our social and political awareness, demands for funding of anti-pollution efforts through tax incentives are inevitable.

Tax expenditures directly for pollution efforts first saw light of day with the suspension of investment credit in 1966. An exception was made, continuing the seven percent investment credit for pollution control facilities during the suspension period. Pollution control facilities also were granted an exception to the repeal of the tax exempt status of industrial development bonds in 1968. Thus it was not too surprising that, when the President recommended repeal of the seven percent investment credit in April, 1969, testimony submitted to the Ways and Means Committee immediately suggested an exception for pollution abatement facilities.

The Treasury and the Department of Health, Education and Welfare opposed any exception to preserve the investment credit for antipollution devices. From the Treasury standpoint, of course, creation of this exception would merely invite other exceptions, and thus erode the effectiveness of repeal as an antiinflationary measure. But Secretary Finch, in a letter to the Committee, spelled out objections to such an exception from the standpoint of the nation's pollution abatement. Since the necessary equipment yields little or no return, alternative uses of funds would be economically more attractive. Hence any "incentive" effect of a tax preference was doubtful. Further, the Department of Health, Education, and Welfare argued, the prime incentive for industry to engage in pollution abatement efforts arises from state and local regulatory requirements. Thus, the tax expenditure was simply paying businesses to do what they would have to do in any event.

Under this analysis the proposal to provide an investment credit for pollution control facilities simply amounted to cost-sharing by the Federal government. The testimony before the Ways and Means Committee by industry representatives confirmed this view. Virtually without exception private industry representatives argued that they were being forced by local regulations to install pollution equipment; the equipment would not increase profits and was being installed for the public good; and therefore the public should bear part of the cost through the mechanism of an investment credit.

Seidman Lectures

Several questions immediately occur. Is the cost sharing really needed? If so, is industrial investment in depreciable hardware the best form of investment for effective pollution control? And, finally, who should properly bear the cost of cleaning up industrial pollution?

Secretary Finch pointed out that the cost to industry of effective pollution control efforts is quite small. A 1967 Report by an interagency Working Committee on Economic Incentives entitled, "Cost Sharing With Industry," concluded that the annual cost of effective air and water pollution abatement would be less than one-half percent of value added by all manufacturing and electric power industries. This relatively small cost did not appear to warrant Federal cost sharing.

The Federal subsidy through the investment credit was also considered an inefficient and, in the long run, possibly undesirable approach to pollution abatement. The investment credit could only be available for investment in end-of-the-line hardware. Thus there would be a marked incentive for businesses to use hardware as a solution to every pollution problem, precluding concentration on changes in fuel, processing techniques, or changes in raw materials utilization, none of which could qualify for Federal tax cost-sharing funds. Technically, these latter approaches appear to offer sounder long range approaches to pollution abatement, and Secretary Finch therefore argued that the tax credit would subsidize the more inefficient and ineffective techniques.

Despite Treasury and Health, Education, and Welfare opposition, and with no substantive supporting study, the Ways and Means Committee voted a special five year rapid amortization provision for certified pollution control facilities. The taxpayer can thus deduct his total cost in five years even though normal tax depreciation rules would establish a longer useful life for the property. While this provision was intended as a substitute for the repeal of the seven percent investment credit, interestingly enough, some long lived equipment would have received a tax benefit from the new rapid write-off provision equal to a twenty percent investment credit. Through this new provision the tax writing committee of the House in effect appropriated $400 million annually to share costs for an effort that from the evidence available needed no subsidy and for an approach that is inefficient and ineffective in the long run. Further, consideration of pollution efforts by the substantive Congressional committees had indicated that the money may be better spent on basic research and directed to state and local government efforts. And, as evidence rises that the pollution efforts must be mounted on a regional basis, the tax incentive becomes even less apt.

Nevertheless, the Senate also adopted this new tax preference, but with changes which cut the annual cost to an estimated $120 million.

The Federal tax expenditure as it emerged in the final bill can be viewed as an interest free loan in the amount of the taxes that would have been paid had normal depreciation been taken for tax purposes during the five year period. Repayment is effected by taking less than normal depreciation in subsequent years. This loan is available only to those corporations that are in a profit position; loss corporations must borrow their funds from commercial sources at prevailing interest rates.

Alternatively, the tax expenditure can be viewed as

a Federal loan program for the full capital cost of the facilities, but at a reduced interest rate. So analyzed, this results in a reduction in the corporation's borrowing costs by some two to three percent, depending on the useful life of the property and the amount the corporation can otherwise earn on its money. Again, the loss corporation receives no reduction in its interest cost; it must pay the going rate of interest.

As a means of financing the antipollution effort, the five year rapid write-off provision shares all the infirmities that Secretary Finch noted with respect to granting an investment credit for pollution abatement facilities. From the standpoint of the tax system, the special provision also produces problems. The corporate tax system does not rely on a progressive rate structure. Nonetheless tax incentives in the corporate system produce inequities just as in the individual tax system.

The fundamental precept of the corporate tax system is that a flat rate of tax will be imposed on corporate net income. Those corporations with the same net income should pay the same tax. But the rapid amortization provision violates this precept. Assume that corporation A has depreciable assets that are not pollution control facilities, and after all deductions, has taxable income of $500,000. Corporation B has an identical cost basis in depreciable assets, but part are certified pollution control facilities. In the absence of the rapid amortization provision, B would have the same taxable income as corporation A and pay the same Federal tax. Solely because of the special tax provision, Corporation B will now pay a lower tax for five years than corporation A. And because the Federal loan is interest free, this represents a permanent financial gain for Corporation B relative to Corporation A.

Thus, under the definition offered above, the rapid write-off provision is a tax expenditure. It creates differing tax results on a basis wholly apart from proper rules for accounting for the cost of producing income. Like other tax expenditures, it is irrational in operation. It assists only profitable polluters; the loss corporation gets no Federal cost sharing because it cannot meet the basic requirement for obtaining the interest free Federal loan, namely profit. Even though a loss corporation might demonstrate that it faced a more serious pollution control problem than its profitable counterpart, it gets no Federal aid through the tax system.

Similarly, large corporations would be entitled to a larger loan relatively than would small corporations. The tax benefit of rapid amortization is only twenty-two percent of the amount written off for a small corporation. A large corporation benefits to the extent of forty-eight percent of its write-off. Again the amount of the government loan has no relation to the problem of pollution control or indeed no necessary correlation to the size of the business operation, since heavy losses could conceivably place a very large business in the lower tax bracket.

Congress, interestingly enough, recognized the adverse impact on tax equity of the new tax preference by providing that the new minimum tax be applied to the excess of rapid amortization over straight line depreciation. The minimum tax might thus be viewed as the interest that the government is charging for its loan. But again the amount and incidence of this "tax interest" are highly arbitrary and erratic in operation. And Congress was sufficiently concerned about the provision to provide an automatic termination date in five years in order to insure review and evaluation of the rule.

Seidman Lectures

Whatever the uneven operation of tax expenditures for pollution abatement, it is clear that the tax expenditure is bottomed on the assumption that the public should bear a significant part of the cost of industrial pollution abatement. Tax expenditure analysis thus brings us to the third question raised above. Who should bear this cost? Industry representatives argued before the Senate Finance Committee that pollution abatement was for the public good; therefore the public should bear the cost. Indeed some proposals for additional tax benefits submitted to the Senate Finance Committee would have resulted in the public bearing over seventy-five percent of the cost of industrial pollution abatement facilities.

The public is already providing cost sharing benefits to industry in programs quite apart from special tax incentives through research, low cost loans and direct grants. Many economists feel that the direct cost of abating industrial pollution should largely be borne by industry. Thus, expenditures for pollution control efforts would either be absorbed by the corporations themselves or passed on to consumers of the industrial products in the form of higher prices. If industry is presently keeping its costs or prices down because it is using the public air and water in a manner that creates pollution, then this economic view should be borne either by investors in the industry in the form of lower profits or by the consumers of the products in the form of higher prices. These are the groups that benefit from the use of the public air and water, and they should absorb the costs of utilizing these natural resources in a manner that does not create an unacceptable level of pollution.

The President's pollution proposals appear to have

accepted this analysis in part. In the proposal for the creation of adequate municipal waste treatment plants, the President has required that Federally funded plants must impose user charges on industries so that the cost of treating industrial waste will be absorbed by industry. In effect this is a decision that, in this program, the general public should not be required to bear the costs of industrial pollution abatement.

Some economists have gone further and called for imposition of effluent charges and emission fees on those industries that create pollution at levels above standards determined to be acceptable. The charges would have to be set at such a level that an industry could not economically afford to continue polluting air or water. In other words, the charges must be so burdensome that industry is required to convert to lower cost pollution abatement practices. The financial burden of industrial pollution control under this plan is placed on industry. Again either the investor or the consumer will bear these costs, with the relative burden that each group absorbs varying from industry to industry. Senator Proxmire has introduced legislation to implement a national system of effluent charges in the case of water pollution. Some localities have tried such a system, apparently with considerable success. One of the advantages claimed for a national system is that it provides financing for concerted regional attacks on pollution, a step which pollution experts now generally consider essential.

From the economists' standpoint, there is considerable agreement that the cost of dealing with industrial pollution is properly placed on industry. Charges for keeping the public air and water clean of industrial pollution are simply a part of the cost of doing business, which costs industry has improperly avoided thus far at the expense of the public.

However, technology and politics have not yet reached a point where the economists' solution can be satisfactorily implemented. Difficult measurement and standards problems must be resolved by those dealing with the technical problems of pollution. Politically, there is yet little agreement on the proper allocation of the cost of controlling industrial pollution between the public and affected industry groups, between the investors and consumers. Further, the contours of effective political action are still evolving to determine the proper roles of Federal, state and local, and regional political authority.

Undoubtedly, these reasons played a part in the President's omission of any mention of effluent charges or emission fees from his pollution control program. For the Council of Economic Advisors and the 1967 Interagency Study Group have both recommended such action as an appropriate step, at least on an experimental basis.

The contours of a substitute for present tax expenditures for pollution control facilities thus do not emerge as clearly from public consideration as is the case with tax provisions affecting charitable giving. The absence of a viable alternative to the tax incentive was reflected in the debate on the Tax Reform Act. Proponents of strong pollution control efforts, such as Senator Muskie, could recognize the adverse impact on the tax laws of the rapid amortization rule. But they saw no alternative available that would insure direction of Federal funds to this high priority social problem. Hence, they opposed any effort to strike this new tax preference from the bill.

Despite the lack of complete clarity, certain features of an alternative approach to the present tax expenditure emerge:

(1) The special provision for rapid amortization of the cost of pollution control facilities in the Tax Reform Act of 1969 should be repealed. It violates the integrity of the corporate tax system and it is an inappropriate and ineffective expenditure of Federal funds for abatement of industrial pollution.

(2) A significant portion of costs of clearing industrial pollution should be absorbed largely by industry and not by the general public, whether through tax or direct expenditures. The present tax incentive is inconsistent with this principle.

(3) The costs of reducing industrial pollution to acceptable levels appear well within the capacity of most industry groups to absorb without undue burden on profits or excessive upward pressure on prices. In the case of loss or marginal profit situations low cost loans could be employed. Tax incentives are again undesirable since they provide maximum aid to industries that need no financial assistance, and little or no aid to those that do.

(4) Economic analysis points to a system of effluent and emission charges, both to control pollution and to help finance the general pollution effort. Here the dimensions of the political and technological response are still unclear. However, the use of tax incentives

appears to offer little assistance in resolving these problems, and more likely will prove a positive hindrance.

(5) Finally, adequate political and financing techniques must be developed if regional approaches to pollution abatement are to be employed.

Tax Expenditures and Housing

The contours of an alternative to tax incentives for charitable donations have emerged with some clarity from tax expenditure analysis. In the case of pollution abatement, the dimensions of an alternative to tax preferences are developing but are not yet in sharp focus. In the final area of social need for consideration — housing — the criteria for an alternative to present tax preferences for real estate investment are shadowy at best. Tax expenditure analysis in this final area so far points mostly in the direction of questions to be considered rather than definitive answers.

Present tax laws contain a number of preferential provisions to encourage the investment in housing. At the level of individual home ownership, of course, the primary tax benefit is the deduction for interest on home mortgages. Mention has previously been made of the upside down affect of this provision, whereby home ownership for the wealthy receives a much greater Federal boost than for the poor. The deduction for local property taxes has a similar effect. By contrast, section 235 of the Federal Housing Act is a program of direct Federal financial assistance to facilitate home ownership by low income families.

Attention on the nation's housing needs has primarily focused on the shortage of low and moderate income rental housing. Programs under section 221 and 236 of the Federal Housing Act are directed specifically at this target group. Several of the provisions in the Tax Reform Act of 1969 reflect a similar concern.

The extent of the housing problem facing the United States cannot be overstated. It has been estimated that there are presently some seventy million housing units in the country. But over seven million of these are classified as substandard. With the recent economic decline in the housing industry, new housing starts are now down to about one million per year. Yet in 1968 the nation accepted a goal of twenty-six million units to be constructed over a ten year period. This failure to provide an adequate supply of decent housing bears most heavily on low and moderate income families.

Much of the discussion during consideration of the Tax Reform Act as to tax provisions affecting real estate arose out of the very legitimate concern that we need to increase the level of Federal funding to encourage development of more low and middle income housing. The Department of Housing and Urban Development therefore campaigned vigorously not only to retain present tax preferences for housing, but to provide new ones for lower income residential property.

Tax reformers shared this concern for the housing problem. But they were also concerned with the inequities the various preferences create in the tax system and seriously questioned whether the tax expenditure approach was an effective and efficient utilization of admittedly limited Federal funds.

The principal tax incentive for investment in rental residential real property is the right to compute the depreciation deduction on one of the permissable accelerated methods, notably the two hundred percent declining balance method. This special provision permits the equity investor to recover much more of his investment in the early years of the life of the property than he otherwise could under normal straight line or sinking fund depreciation. The Tax Reform Act retained this privilege for investment in residential housing, while cutting back on the benefits of accelerated depreciation for nonresidential real property. Quite obviously, the intent of Congress was to encourage increased investment in housing.

The difficulty in the Congressional action lies in the effects of the tax incentive. The incentive is confined in its direct impact to the investor group. No direct benefit is conferred on the other members of the typical real estate quadriad: the developer, the financing institution, and the tenants. Renters, for example, get no tax benefit equivalent to the deductions for interest and property taxes available to homeowners.

But even within the investor group accelerated depreciation has the inverted effect we have noted for other tax incentive provisions. That is, the tax provision is more beneficial to the person who presumably needs it least — the wealthy taxpayer. Here the high-bracket individual uses the artificially high deduction in the early years of his investment to create a "tax loss" to shelter his other income from tax. For example, the 1968 Treasury Studies on Tax Reform revealed that, out of a group of thirteen wealthy real estate investors, nine paid no Federal income tax and two reduced their tax liability to less than $25, due to the depreciation deduction. One taxpayer with $7.5 million in income over a seven year period paid an effective rate of tax of only eleven percent. It is true that the investor using accelerated depreciation will pay theoretically more taxes in later years as his depreciation falls below what it normally would have been under conventional depreciation methods. But the net effect of this transaction is a loan by the government in the early years in the amount of the tax saving. This loan is repaid by the higher taxes in later years, but the loan bears no interest. And if the investor continues to expand his investments in real estate, the loan itself may never be repaid.

The value of an interest free loan varies directly with the taxpayer's bracket, the useful life of the property, and the rate of return the taxpayer could expect if he invested in other property. But take for example two taxpayers who can each earn ten percent on their money, and who each invest in the same apartment house. One investor is in the thirty percent bracket and one in the seventy percent bracket. The Federal government will through the tax system insure a more profitable investment to the higher bracket investor than to the lower.

If the accelerated depreciation provision were recast as a direct loan program, the resulting statute would provide that the Department of Housing and Urban Affairs is authorized to loan funds to seventy percent bracket taxpayers at a lower rate of interest than would be available to borrowers in the lower brackets. It is difficult to conceive that the Department of Housing and Urban Affairs would urge Congress to enact such a system directly, but its sponsorship of tax incentives produced the same result.

The provision for accelerated depreciation suffers other defects when viewed as a program to solve low income housing needs. It is equally available for investors in luxury housing. Standing alone, therefore, the provision would seem to offer little inducement for investors to enter the low income housing field. Problems of neighborhood deterioration, collection problems, and high property taxes would appear to create a strong bias for opting to invest in high income housing since the benefits of accelerated depreciation are equally available.

Further, the present tax provision permits no direction of Federal funds to areas of greatest need. Creation of additional houses in New York City — when the occupancy rate is less than one percent — gets no higher priority than housing development in areas of the country with less acute housing needs.

Another problem with the use of accelerated depreciation as an incentive for housing investment is the difficulty in ascertaining who does or should ultimately benefit from this expenditure. Does the tax preference simply operate as a floor on the profit margin of the investor? Or is it reflected in part in lower rents than would otherwise be charged, so that tenants may be said to derive some benefit? In either case, just how much money is the government putting into each transaction? Would Congress authorize a direct financial assistance program to either group that has the same features as the present tax expenditure program?

Other difficult questions must be resolved. Does accelerated depreciation simply constitute a windfall to the investor group? Some experts in the housing field assert that no incentive at all is needed to attract capital to the real estate field. Market demand is sufficient to generate the needed funds. Rather, they insist, the real problems inhibiting development of an adequate housing supply are to be found in inequitable property tax structures, zoning regulations, and local building codes. To the extent this analysis is correct, of course, we are misallocating funds by rewarding actions that investors would have taken in any event and diverting funds from other priority areas. Further study and analysis are needed to shed light on this question.

Closely related is the question as to which group in the typical real estate transaction Federal financial aid should be directed. Typically the housing development transaction will involve four parties: the builder, the financier, the equity investor group, and the tenants. To which of these parties should Federal aid be directed if we are to make most efficient use of available Federal funds? Should financial aid be given to builders to reduce building costs? Should programs be expanded to encourage and assist lending institutions to make low cost loans available? If so, to whom? To the builder? To the investors? Or should we concentrate on assisting the tenant group through, for example, rent subsidies?

Whatever answer, or combination of answers, that might be developed, it seems clear that the present tax expenditures of some $250 million per year through accelerated depreciation is a clumsy and inefficient vehicle that falls far short of the sophistication in approach that appears essential.

Given this situation, it was not encouraging that Congress and the Administration recommended continuing down the path of tax expenditures in the Tax Reform Bill as a means of meeting our low income housing needs. For example, the Treasury proposed a special five year rapid amortization provision for rehabilitation of low and moderate income housing. This provision is similar in operation to that provided for investment in pollution control facilities.

This provision illustrates clearly the inadvisability of implementing national housing policy through the tax writing committees of Congress. It is estimated that, under this provision, some $330 million of Federal funds will now be committed to rehabilitation expenditures. Yet, the Department of Housing and Urban Affairs apparently has placed so low a priority on rehabilitation that it has never recommended to the Congress that funds be directly appropriated for this purpose. And indeed it is obvious that rehabilitation is not going to produce the twenty-six million new housing units that we need. There were absolutely no studies made to determine the extent of any rehabilitation need, or, if such a need exists, that the lack of funds is the primary factor affecting failure to rehabilitate dilapidated housing. Nonetheless, through the tax expenditure route, several hundred million dollars in Federal funds will now be diverted to a low priority need.

From the standpoint of tax policy, the rehabilitation tax preference suffers from all the defects of any tax incentive. Testimony before the Senate Finance Committee pointed out that the rehabilitation provision, viewed as a loan program, has the effect of reducing a seventy percent bracket taxpayer's interest costs from eight percent to three percent on property with a twenty year life (assuming a ten percent discount rate). On the other hand, a twenty percent bracket taxpayer would have his interest costs on a similar investment reduced by only one point. It is again almost impossible to conceive that Congress would approve a direct interest subsidy plan with these effects; but through the back door of the tax laws we now have just such a program.

In sum, then, Congress through the rehabilitation provision has instituted a $330 million program that has not been shown to have any rational relation to the shortage of low income housing, but which has obvious deleterious effects on the fairness of the Federal income tax system. A point of considerable irony is added when it is noted that after the Treasury had proposed this provision, it then felt that the benefits flowing from the rapid write off should be included as a tax preference for purposes of the minimum tax. Thus, in a single bill, we have Congressional enactment of a tax preference which, in another provision, it declares to be of unacceptable magnitude! Senator Gore attacked the rapid amortization provisions on the Senate floor during debate of the tax reform bill and attempted to strike them from the bill. Here again, however, advocates of housing programs felt that this was an attack on the nation's commitment to meet this critical social need. These Senators thus opposed deleting these provisions from the bill, although it was pointed out that the effort to remove the unfair tax provision in no way precluded Congress from taking the tax monies so saved and appropriating them directly for housing needs in a rational manner consistent with national priorities.

There are also new provisions in the Tax Reform Act designed to provide greater tax incentives for investing in the so-called limited dividend housing programs under sections 221 and 236 of the Federal Housing Act. These programs are designed to produce low income housing by limiting the investor's return to six percent. Rents are thus maintained at low levels. Opponents of any changes in the rules relating to accelerated depreciation argued that the tax benefits to the investor were taken into account in arriving at the six percent figure. This argument may be correct but, if so, it is certainly difficult to ascertain the rational basis for the limited dividend provisions. For, if the tax benefits were determinative, why is a six percent return proper for the thirty percent taxpayer, who gets less tax benefit and hence a lower profit margin, as well as for the seventy percent taxpayer who derives a greater tax benefit from the depreciation deduction? Put another way, one wonders if opponents of any change really believe that Congress consciously adopted the principle that the seventy percent bracket taxpayer is entitled to a higher rate of return, taking into account the tax benefit plus the statutory six percent, than the thirty percent bracket investor.

Further, one wondered why, if the tax benefit were determinative, it would not be more rational to revise the six percent upward, or provide direct Federal grants to investors to insure an adequate return on their investment.

The Department of Housing and Urban Affairs, rather than considering these alternatives, not only resisted any change in the tax laws but vigorously pushed for further tax benefits for investors in limited dividend housing projects. This action was even more curious in light of the fact that even under existing tax rules, the Department of Housing and Urban Affairs had far more applications for low income housing projects than it could fund with available direct appropriations. But Congress accepted the Department of Housing and Urban Affairs' position. Thus, rules as to recapture of accelerated depreciation are now more liberal for investments in low income housing projects than for other real estate ventures. And a person can defer any recognition of gain at all if he sells one low income housing project to the tenants or to a tax exempt organization and reinvests the proceeds in another. The maximum sales price on these Government-assisted housing projects is the amount of the investor's equity plus the amount of any mortgage and the taxes payable as the result of the sales. The theory of the new tax provision is that the purchase price to occupants of low income housing will be reduced since there will be no Federal income taxes due if the investors will reinvest in another similar project.

Again the tax approach has very curious results. For example, assume two projects in each of which the respective investor has $100,000 equity, $100,000 mortgage, and would recognize a $50,000 gain on sale of the property. Assume that investor A is in the seventy percent bracket and investor B is in the fifty percent bracket. In the absence of the new provision the tenants of investor A would have to pay $235,000 for their property, and the tenants of investor B would pay $225,000. Under the new rule, the occupants of invester A's project could get a $35,000 reduction in their purchase price, whereas investor B's tenants get only a $25,000 price reduction. In a rational world, it may be that these two occupant groups should pay the same price, but that result would not likely be predicated on the amount of total income that the investor happened to earn.

As in the areas of social concerns already considered, present tax incentive policy to encourage development of housing assumes very strange dimensions when viewed as a Federal expenditure policy. And present tax rules constitute a serious deviation from tax equity. A start was made in modifying the magnitude of the disequity in the Tax Reform Act. But only a start. And again, it was the failure of tax reformers to have a viable alternative to the present tax expenditure system that

Seidman Lectures

prevented further tax reform. For, those whose task it is to promote our national housing policies felt they had no alternative but to fight for the tax preferences if they were offered no other avenue by which the same amount of Federal funds would be made available for low and middle income housing. An inefficient and erratic expenditure funding system was viewed as preferable to losing funds represented by tax expenditures altogether.

When one tries to analyze the dimensions of an alternative system, the considerations that should be controlling are not at all clear. Primarily the cloudiness of the picture is caused by the lack of information with respect to the certain fundamental questions already noted. How much does the Federal government contribute to a given housing project under the present tax system? How much should the government contribute to induce developers and investors to enter the housing area? To financiers? To tenants? Should the financial aid be focused on a particular segment of the housing quadriad, or in some combination? What are the sources of our failures to provide adequate low income housing through the private sector? Does the problem lie in lack of adequate capital, uncertainty of return, local taxing and regulatory policies, tenant relation problems, or in some combination of them? What form of financial contribution should the government make if these factors can be analyzed? Direct grants? Low interest or interest free loans? Guarantees?

We do not now have adequate answers to these questions. This situation makes it even more undesirable to use the tax mechanism, since we do know that the tax incentive provisions are harmful to a fair tax system. But until we have the answers to these kinds of questions, it will be difficult, if not impossible, to convince Congress and those responsible for adequately housing our people that tax reform can proceed further in eliminating tax preferences for real estate.

Conclusion

The tax expenditure concept is a highly useful analytical tool in evaluating the impact, effectiveness, and efficiency of tax incentive provisions. This discussion has centered on tax incentives for charitable giving, pollution control facilities, and housing. But it is equally applicable to the tax provisions for depletion allowances, intangible drilling expenses, deductions for state and local taxes and medical expenses, and the myriad other provisions in the tax code that have been inserted to achieve nontax purposes.

Tax expenditures cannot be effected without doing violence to the integrity of the tax system. If, as I believe, a progressive individual income tax system mirrors values to which our society is deeply committed, then proposals to distort that system must be vigorously resisted and we must continue to press for removal of those provisions now in the law that violate the integrity of our tax system.

But tax reformers must constantly bear in mind the validity of the values that underlie the calls for utilizing the tax system to meet social goals. These values conflict with those inherent in a progressive tax system whenever the tax system is used to solve the social problems. This potential conflict is resolved one way or another within our political system. If defenders of the tax system have no viable alternatives for financing programs for meeting pressing social needs outside the tax system, then political realities will inevitably dictate a compromise. This compromise usually will mean that the tax system will be distorted — but not as much as proposed. And social needs will receive some Federal funds — but not as much nor as effectively spent as desired. As those compromises pyramid over the years, the confidence of the taxpayer erodes a little bit with each deviation, however small, in tax equity. The problem is that social needs that can only be met with Federal funds must rely on the tax system to collect the bulk of those funds. If public confidence in that tax system is continuously eroded — albeit ostensibly to achieve highly praiseworthy social or economic objectives — then we may truly face a "taxpayers' revolt," and social needs will not be met, either by direct or by tax expenditures.

"How Can We Kick The Intaxication Habit"

Lecture Three

by J. S. Seidman

It is fitting that we have this discussion so close to April 15, the day when our income really becomes a collector's item. In the two lectures you have had this year, Dr. Heller showed you how taxes civilize us and Mr. McDaniel showed you how taxes agonize us. The burden of my song is that taxes pulverize us.

Taxes and liquor have a great deal in common. They are both habit forming. Too much liquor leads to intoxication; and too much tax leads to intaxication. It is the too much part of the habit that we must kick.

How are we going to do that? That's the problem that besets us. My answer will touch on a few of the highspots and then with tremendous over-simplification. This is sure to leave questions and doubts in your minds. Perhaps during the question and comment period we can close the gap.

Let us first take a look at the amount of intaxication. I suppose to measure the amount of intaxication we ought to do it in terms of pints, fifths, or quarts; but let me indulge in a few numbers. The cost of government is equal to $1600 a year for every person in this country. That gives us the dubious distinction of having the most expensive government in the world per individual. I have a feeling that we ought to stop calling them cheap politicians! We're supposed to be a government of checks and balances. We issue plenty of checks and have mighty few balances.

Taxes take one-third of everything we produce. The average American worker spends more for taxes than for any other single item in the family budget. One-third of the time and the talent of this nation goes for taxes. It also means that we are one-third socialized. For those of you who are looking for some consolation in the last part, you need not worry about the Russians ever burying us. We're doing a mighty good job on ourselves. Mind I said nothing whatsoever about inflation which certainly is a form of taxation that adds to the burial process.

What is the result of all this intaxication? The high toll of taxes is that taxes rather than common sense run our personal and our business lives. Just look at what we have permitted the tax laws to do to us.

Taxes dictate what we do with our time and our money while we are around, and what we say in our wills for the hereafter. Taxes play a very significant role in determining whether we work, how much we work, when and where we work. Taxes even enter into such intimate matters as whether we marry, whom we marry, when we marry — and how we marry.

Certainly the stock market is steeped in taxes, and these taxes have a great influence in determining what we buy, and when we sell.

In business, taxes rather than the marketplace are the kingpin in determining: whether we do business as a proprietorship, partnership, or corporation; whether we have one or more companies; whether we capitalize these companies with stock or debt or both; whether we pay dividends and how much we pay; whether we liquidate, sell, or stay put. In a word, taxes are distorting our economy and our humanity.

What's behind all this? At least three things are out of gear — certainly as applied to the federal income tax which is the largest and the most pervasive tax of the lot. The three are: (1) the rates are too high, (2) there are too many loopholes, and (3) the laws are too complicated.

I mentioned rates first because they are arch enemy number one. Personal rates go skyward above seventy percent. No wonder we sometimes refer to the Eternal Revenue Service! Human nature rebels at the fantastic tax rates. And the rebellion takes the form of either trying to beat the game, or not playing it at all. That's hardly a compliment to our moral fabric.

Furthermore, when taxes pluck off seventy percent or more of our income, we're in the weird situation where there is over three times more to be gained by saving a dollar of tax than in earning a dollar of income. That necessarily produces a tremendous drain of thought and energy devoted to taxes that could otherwise be put to more productive use.

Why then are the rates so high? One reason is the doodads that are in the law. Let me explain that. What I call doodads are generally known as loopholes. And what we call loopholes are often nothing more than special provisions deliberately put into the law by Congress to apologize for the high tax rates. They are Congress' way of making the law more palatable for some groups by giving them escape hatches.

The trouble is that when we let one group off the hook, the others must pick up the tab. The taxpayers who are not benefitted by these doodads feel they are entitled to some relief as well. And so they help themselves to all sorts of gimmicks. It is intriguing to find that even the dullest minds can make the cleverest deductions.

I said that our laws are too complicated. That's one phase on which I imagine all of us will agree. The philosophy upon which the laws seem to be written is that if you can't convince them, confuse them. They contain every earmark of a conspiracy in restraint of understanding.

Among rates, loopholes, and complications, we find outselves reeling from intaxication. If we want to sober up, obviously we have to cut down on the bottle. How do we do that?

At the onset we must recognize, as we put taxes on the couch, that taxes are not a cause, but an effect. The cause is spending. Our governments are now spending over three hundred billion dollars a year. Who said man wants little here below?

Someone has to pay that three hundred billion dollar bill. The only way that government can pay to people is to take from people. That means three hundred billion dollars in taxes.

It is idle to talk about who should pay, because whoever pays is maintaining the habit, whereas we want to kick it. To kick it, we must cut that three hundred billion dollar dosage way down. How do we do that?

First I submit a general proposition, and then I will outline several of its specifics. The general proposition is

Seidman Lectures

that we are going at government spending in a topsy-turvy way. We should not start with what the government says it needs, but rather what it is that we can afford to spend. This is the way we prepare our personal budgets. Government ought to be handled in the same way.

Parkinson's laws should always ring in our ears, that expenditures rise to meet income. The best way to close the door on spending is not to open the door on the money. Oliver Wendell Holmes put it this way: "Keep the government poor and remain free."

How do we determine how much we can afford to spend? That ought not to be left to politicking or to chance. Instead there should be a pre-set formula for doing this. One logical way would be a fixed percentage of the national product or the national income. The resulting figure would be "it." The "it" would be the government's ceiling on expenditures for that year, with no ifs, ands, or buts.

If the government had planned to spend more than that amount, the items would have to be lined up in the order of their importance, and cut off at the spending limit. That's the general approach.

Now let's see how we can take some specific whacks at the three hundred billion dollars. The biggest slice of the three hundred billion dollars is the cost of man's warring. Whether that can be whittled down or not, and how, I'm going to pass by, or else we may start another war in this auditorium or around it. Besides, there is plenty of pay dirt to extract from the non-war expenditures.

President Eisenhower repeatedly called to our attention that the government is engaged in business where it has no business being. Since President Eisenhower's time we have gone further down that road, not less. The government is steeped today in well over seven hundred different businesses cutting across the commercial, industrial, and financial spectrum. These businesses are not the sort of thing that government alone can best do at the lowest cost, or with the least side effects. In the hands of government, these businesses are not moneymakers, but money-takers.

Look at the magic that would be wrought by getting the government out of these businesses. The sale of their assets would yield eighty billion dollars. Eighty billion dollars is enough to liquidate one quarter of the total federal debt, and eliminate four billion dollars of annual expenditures for interest.

Furthermore the huge annual losses that are now being sustained by these businesses would be eliminated from the three hundred billion dollars. Instead, in private hands, those businesses would become taxpayers. By getting the government out of these businesses there could be a dramatic kicking of the tax habit by billions of dollars.

Let us take another area: spendings that go at cross-purposes with one another. We have a huge set of spending that goes in one direction, and another huge set that goes in just the opposite direction. For example, we spend millions of dollars to reclaim farmlands. But we also spend billions of dollars to pay farmers not to produce on their farmlands. We spend millions of dollars to keep prices down, as in the regulation of utility rates, rent controls and so on. We also spend millions of dollars, in fact billions of dollars, in price supports to keep prices up.

The economic effect of these expenditures is to cancel each other out. In a sense they are a nullity. We have played both sides of the spending street. That is a costly habit that we just must kick.

Next we have the costly overlap in the vast number of taxing authorities that exist. We have one federal government, and we have fifty states. Those two basic groups are fine. When we get to the third basic group — the localities — we find that there are eighty-seven thousand units that have taxing authority. Furthermore, these units subdivide into additional taxing districts. All told, there are a hundred and seventy-five thousand taxing agencies. Each of these has its own personnel, its own space, its own equipment, its own forms, its own procedures.

Then, to confound and compound the problem, many of these units impose the same type of tax but with far different laws and far different procedures. That alone is enough to drive taxpayers to drink, and bring on the very intaxication that we are trying to cure.

Tremendous forward strides could be made if one basic group had exclusive command over a particular type of tax. For example, the federal government alone could have jurisdiction over the income tax, the states alone could impose a sales tax, and the localities alone could impose a property tax. In other words, sharp pruning of the number of taxing agencies and restricting them to a certain type of tax should be able to kick billions out of that three hundred billion dollars.

I referred earlier to the complications of the laws. Additional billions could be saved by eliminating them. Aside from the fact that our entire tax system is endangered by these complications, their cost is tremendous to both government and taxpayer. To government there is the cost of researching, drafting, enacting, administering, and adjudicating these complications. To the taxpayer, there is the cost of becoming acquainted with the provisions, preparing the returns, dealing with audits, and settling controversies.

A study was made by the National Industrial Conference Board several years ago on this very topic. The Board estimated that the taxpayer's cost was at least three percent of the tax. Three percent of the tax today is nine billion dollars a year. The government's cost is certainly no less than that. And so we can sober up many billions of dollars' worth if we rid ourselves of the laws' ambiguities and complications.

How do we do that? I am going to make a highly revolutionary proposal on one aspect of the complication problem. My suggestion is that we write the tax laws in English! It's old hat to say that our tax system stands or falls on taxpayer goodwill and voluntary compliance. But it is not old hat to point out that with the best will, to comply a taxpayer must understand what it is that he is supposed to comply with. Yet in all too many places in the tax law, experts cannot make head nor tail of the grammar of some of the provisions, no less their meaning. Pity the plight of the poor, unsophisticated taxpayer.

The problems to be dealt with *are* complex. We are a complex society with dynamic fertile-minded taxpayers. But while the areas are complex, the language used to deal with them need not be.

After all, educational television has found it possible to explain such complicated subjects as the moonshot, atomic energy, and photosynthesis so that the public can understand them. By the same token, it should be possible to write the tax script so that the taxpayers know the rules of the game. Simplicity and clarity have billions of dollars of premium value in kicking the intaxication habit.

Next, I recommend that we have another Hoover-type of check-up on government. It's over twenty years since the original Hoover Commission. Its ideas yielded an estimated savings of nearly four billion dollars a year. I submit that it is high time that we took another look.

The look should not be confined, as it was originally, to the federal government. It should include the states and localities. All these governments have grown considerably in the last twenty years. My guess is that a Hoover Commission would now be able to slash spendings several times the four billion dollars of twenty years ago.

To summarize, my program to kick the intaxication habit is this:

(1) Determine through a pre-set formula the amount of government spending that we can afford, and limit taxes to that amount.
(2) Get government out of private business and out of its huge loss.
(3) Eliminate all expenditures that conflict with one another.
(4) Prune sharply the number of taxing agencies and the type of tax they can impose.
(5) Write the tax laws in clear English.
(6) Have another Hoover Commission study of government.
(7) And then to see to it that none of this program is undermined, designate a spending and taxing ombudsman to maintain the necessary vigil.

If we did all this, how much spending would be eliminated? My estimate is a guesstimate and a wild one at that. I can see the possibilities of cutting back by sixty billion dollars. Sixty billion dollars is twenty percent of all government spending. That means twenty percent of all the taxes that are being imposed today.

Those are the possibilities. How do we convert them to realities? Will the legislators do it on their own? I doubt it. Why? In a democracy, although it is by far the best form of government, it is not reasonable to expect any legislature voluntarily to eliminate any expenditure that can vote! To put it another way, we probably cannot muster enough statesmen who are ready to risk or commit political suicide to do what is right for the long run as against what is politically wise for the next election.

On the other hand, legislators will heed anything they sense the public really wants. They know that if they are to continue being legislators they cannot long vote things that do not have public support. In the last analysis, responsibility for spending and taxes gets right down to the people — as it should in a democracy.

Do we really want to kick the intaxication habit? It is natural for all of us to want a tax cut. But it is also natural for us to want to be in on the receiving side of government spending. Obviously we cannot have it both ways.

I have already said that the road to tax reduction is through expenditure reduction. Lip service and pious resolutions do not bring about expenditure cuts. If we really want expenditure reduction, we must be ready to clamp down on expenditures where our own hand is in the till. The acid test is whether we are ready to fight for the elimination of an expenditure that today benefits us personally. We must be that serious about kicking the intaxication habit.

If we are, there are these new ten commandments to be heeded:

(1) We must realize that today's promises are tomorrow's taxes.
(2) We must therefore turn a deaf ear to rosy pictures of lavish spending programs that we just cannot afford.
(3) We must stop trying to get the most and give the least; featherbedding of any sort threatens our economy and our jobs.
(4) We must therefore have an interest in work, a pride in work, and a sense of responsibility toward work.
(5) We must recognize that nothing impoverishes us more than paying a dollar without getting a dollar's worth in return.
(6) We must therefore insist that government condition every expenditure on getting its money's worth.
(7) We must call for the same tough yardsticks for public expenditures as for private expenditures.
(8) We must require that priorities be assigned to planned expenditures, to permit postponement or elimination as need be.
(9) We must bring to our tax laws simplicity, equity, certainty, and administrability.
(10) We must get away from the present situation where taxes run our lives instead of the other way around.

These ten commandments can keep us off the shoals of intaxication. If we break them, we get that much closer to falling on evil days.

I want to make this clear. No matter which way we cut it, our tax bill will be large because our problems at home and abroad are large. But taxes need not be as high as they are today, if we really apply sober thinking and determination. Otherwise we as a nation, like so many before us, may stagger and go down because our staggering taxes did not go down.

Maybe I ought not to leave you with that dismal and disturbing thought. Let me cheer you up with something Adam Smith, the great classical economist, once said: "taxes are the badge of a democracy." If taxes are the badge of a democracy, I can assure you that our country is safe for democracy for a long, long time and we are going to have a mighty big badge to show it.

LIBRARY OF DAVIDSON COLLEGE

Books on regular loan may be checked out for **two weeks.** Books must be presented at the Circulation Desk in order to be renewed.

A fine of **five cents** a day is charged after date due.

Special books are subject to special regulations at the discretion of library staff.

NOV. 21. 1974						
JAN. 13. 1978						